Tefal EasyFry & Grill Air Fryer
Cookbook For Beginners

1200 Days of Delicious, Easy and Fast Tefal EasyFry & Grill Air Fryer Recipes to Make Your Life Easy and Making Delicious Meals

for Your Family and Friends

Sofia Ragland

CONTENTS

Beef , pork & Lamb Recipes 54

Fish And Seafood Recipes 67

Bread And Breakfast Recipes

Pancake For Two

Servings:2
Cooking Time: 30 Minutes
Ingredients:
- 1 cup blanched finely ground almond flour
- 2 tablespoons granular erythritol
- 1 tablespoon salted butter, melted
- 1 large egg
- ⅓ cup unsweetened almond milk
- ½ teaspoon vanilla extract

Directions:
1. In a large bowl, mix all ingredients together, then pour half the batter into an ungreased 6" round nonstick baking dish.
2. Place dish into air fryer basket. Adjust the temperature to 320°F and set the timer for 15 minutes. The pancake will be golden brown on top and firm, and a toothpick inserted in the center will come out clean when done. Repeat with remaining batter.
3. Slice in half in dish and serve warm.

Cheddar Soufflés

Servings:4
Cooking Time: 12 Minutes
Ingredients:
- 3 large eggs, whites and yolks separated
- ¼ teaspoon cream of tartar
- ½ cup shredded sharp Cheddar cheese
- 3 ounces cream cheese, softened

Directions:
1. In a large bowl, beat egg whites together with cream of tartar until soft peaks form, about 2 minutes.
2. In a separate medium bowl, beat egg yolks, Cheddar, and cream cheese together until frothy, about 1 minute. Add egg yolk mixture to whites, gently folding until combined.
3. Pour mixture evenly into four 4" ramekins greased with cooking spray. Place ramekins into air fryer basket. Adjust the temperature to 350°F and set the timer for 12 minutes. Eggs will be browned on the top and firm in the center when done. Serve warm.

Protein Egg Cups

Servings: 4
Cooking Time: 9 Minutes
Ingredients:
- 3 eggs, lightly beaten
- 4 tomato slices
- 4 tsp cheddar cheese, shredded
- 2 bacon slices, cooked and crumbled
- Pepper
- Salt

Directions:
1. Spray silicone muffin molds with cooking spray.
2. In a small bowl, whisk the egg with pepper and salt.
3. Preheat the air fryer to 350°F.
4. Pour eggs into the silicone muffin molds. Divide cheese and bacon into molds.
5. Top each with tomato slice and place in the air fryer basket.
6. Cook for 9 minutes.
7. Serve and enjoy.

Flaky Cinnamon Rolls

Servings:8
Cooking Time: 12 Minutes Per Batch
Ingredients:
- 1 sheet frozen puff pastry, thawed
- 6 tablespoons unsalted butter, melted
- ¾ cup granulated sugar
- 2 tablespoons ground cinnamon
- ½ cup confectioners' sugar
- 2 tablespoons heavy cream

Directions:
1. Preheat the air fryer to 320°F. Cut parchment paper to fit the air fryer basket.
2. Unroll puff pastry into a large rectangle. Brush with butter, then evenly sprinkle sugar and cinnamon around dough, coating as evenly as possible.
3. Starting at one of the long sides, roll dough into a log, then use a little water on your fingers to seal the edge.
4. Slice dough into eight rounds. Place on parchment in the air fryer basket, working in batches as necessary, and cook 12 minutes until golden brown and flaky. Let cool 5 minutes.
5. In a small bowl, whisk confectioners' sugar and cream together until smooth. Drizzle over cinnamon rolls and serve.

Smoked Fried Tofu

Servings: 2
Cooking Time:22 Minutes
Ingredients:
- 1 tofu block; pressed and cubed
- 1 tbsp. smoked paprika
- 1/4 cup cornstarch
- Salt and black pepper to the taste
- Cooking spray

Directions:
1. Grease your air fryer's basket with cooking spray and heat the fryer at 370°F.
2. In a bowl; mix tofu with salt, pepper, smoked paprika and cornstarch and toss well.
3. Add tofu to you air fryer's basket and cook for 12 minutes shaking the fryer every 4 minutes. Divide into bowls and serve for breakfast.

Ham And Egg Toast Cups

Servings:2
Cooking Time:5 Minutes
Ingredients:
- 2 eggs
- 2 slices of ham
- 2 tablespoons butter
- Cheddar cheese, for topping
- Salt, to taste
- Black pepper, to taste

Directions:
1. Preheat the Air fryer to 400°F and grease both ramekins with melted butter.
2. Place each ham slice in the greased ramekins and crack each egg over ham slices.
3. Sprinkle with salt, black pepper and cheddar cheese and transfer into the Air fryer basket.
4. Cook for about 5 minutes and remove the ramekins from the basket.
5. Serve warm.

Sausage Egg Muffins

Servings: 4
Cooking Time: 30 Minutes
Ingredients:
- 6 oz Italian sausage
- 6 eggs
- 1/8 cup heavy cream
- 3 oz cheese

Directions:
1. Preheat the fryer to 350°F.

2. Grease a muffin pan.
3. Slice the sausage links and place them two to a tin.
4. Beat the eggs with the cream and season with salt and pepper.
5. Pour over the sausages in the tin.
6. Sprinkle with cheese and the remaining egg mixture.
7. Cook for 20 minutes or until the eggs are done and serve!

Zucchini And Spring Onions Cakes

Servings: 4
Cooking Time: 8 Minutes
Ingredients:
- 8 ounces zucchinis, chopped
- 2 spring onions, chopped
- 2 eggs, whisked
- Salt and black pepper to the taste
- ¼ teaspoon sweet paprika, chopped
- Cooking spray

Directions:
1. In a bowl, mix all the ingredients except the cooking spray, stir well and shape medium fritters out of this mix. Put the basket in the Air Fryer, add the fritters inside, grease them with cooking spray and cook at 400°F for 8 minutes. Divide the fritters between plates and serve for breakfast.

Simple Egg Soufflé

Servings: 2
Cooking Time: 8 Minutes
Ingredients:
- 2 eggs
- 1/4 tsp chili pepper
- 2 tbsp heavy cream
- 1/4 tsp pepper
- 1 tbsp parsley, chopped
- Salt

Directions:
1. In a bowl, whisk eggs with remaining gradients.
2. Spray two ramekins with cooking spray.
3. Pour egg mixture into the prepared ramekins and place into the air fryer basket.
4. Cook soufflé at 390°F for 8 minutes.
5. Serve and enjoy.

Sausage-crusted Egg Cups

Servings:6
Cooking Time: 15 Minutes
Ingredients:

- 12 ounces ground pork breakfast sausage
- 6 large eggs
- ½ teaspoon salt
- ¼ teaspoon ground black pepper
- ½ teaspoon crushed red pepper flakes

Directions:

1. Place sausage in six 4" ramekins greased with cooking oil. Press sausage down to cover bottom and about ½" up the sides of ramekins. Crack one egg into each ramekin and sprinkle evenly with salt, black pepper, and red pepper flakes.
2. Place ramekins into air fryer basket. Adjust the temperature to 350°F and set the timer for 15 minutes. Egg cups will be done when sausage is fully cooked to at least 145°F and the egg is firm. Serve warm.

Eggs Salad

Servings: 4
Cooking Time: 10 Minutes
Ingredients:

- 1 tablespoon lime juice
- 4 eggs, hard boiled, peeled and sliced
- 2 cups baby spinach
- Salt and black pepper to the taste
- 3 tablespoons heavy cream
- 2 tablespoons olive oil

Directions:

1. In your Air Fryer, mix the spinach with cream, eggs, salt and pepper, cover and cook at 360°F for 6 minutes. Transfer this to a bowl, add the lime juice and oil, toss and serve for breakfast.

Buttery Scallops

Servings: 2
Cooking Time: 8 Minutes
Ingredients:

- 1 lb jumbo scallops
- 1 tbsp fresh lemon juice
- 2 tbsp butter, melted

Directions:

1. Preheat the air fryer to 400°F.
2. In a small bowl, mix together lemon juice and butter.
3. Brush scallops with lemon juice and butter mixture and place into the air fryer basket.

4. Cook scallops for 4 minutes. Turn halfway through.
5. Again brush scallops with lemon butter mixture and cook for 4 minutes more. Turn halfway through.
6. Serve and enjoy.

Egg In A Hole

Servings: 4
Cooking Time: 10 Minutes
Ingredients:

- 4 slices white sandwich bread
- 4 large eggs
- ½ teaspoon salt
- ¼ teaspoon ground black pepper

Directions:

1. Preheat the air fryer to 350°F. Spray a 6" round cake pan with cooking spray.
2. Place as many pieces of bread as will fit in one layer in prepared pan, working in batches as necessary.
3. Using a small cup or cookie cutter, cut a circle out of the center of each bread slice. Crack an egg directly into each cutout and sprinkle eggs with salt and pepper.
4. Cook 5 minutes, then carefully turn and cook an additional 5 minutes or less, depending on your preference. Serve warm.

Chocolate-hazelnut Bear Claws

Servings:4
Cooking Time: 10 Minutes
Ingredients:

- 1 sheet frozen puff pastry dough, thawed
- 1 large egg, beaten
- ½ cup chocolate-hazelnut spread
- 1 tablespoon confectioners' sugar
- 1 tablespoon sliced almonds

Directions:

1. Preheat the air fryer to 320°F.
2. Unfold puff pastry and cut into four equal squares.
3. Brush egg evenly over puff pastry.
4. To make each bear claw, spread 2 tablespoons chocolate-hazelnut spread over a pastry square. Fold square horizontally to form a triangle and cut four evenly spaced slits about halfway through the top of folded square. Repeat with remaining spread and pastry squares.
5. Sprinkle confectioners' sugar and almonds over bear claws and place directly in the air fryer basket. Cook 10 minutes until puffy and golden brown. Serve warm.

Eggplant Parmesan Subs

Servings: 2
Cooking Time: 13 Minutes
Ingredients:
- 4 Peeled eggplant slices
- Olive oil spray
- 2 tablespoons plus 2 teaspoons Jarred pizza sauce, any variety except creamy
- ¼ cup (about ⅔ ounce) Finely grated Parmesan cheese
- 2 Small, long soft rolls, such as hero, hoagie, or Italian sub rolls (gluten-free, if a concern), split open lengthwise

Directions:
1. Preheat the air fryer to 350°F .
2. When the machine is at temperature, coat both sides of the eggplant slices with olive oil spray. Set them in the basket in one layer and air-fry undisturbed for 10 minutes, until lightly browned and softened.
3. Increase the machine's temperature to 375°F. Top each eggplant slice with 2 teaspoons pizza sauce, then 1 tablespoon cheese. Air-fry undisturbed for 2 minutes, or until the cheese has melted.
4. Use a nonstick-safe spatula, and perhaps a flatware fork for balance, to transfer the eggplant slices cheese side up to a cutting board. Set the roll(s) cut side down in the basket in one layer and air-fry undisturbed for 1 minute, to toast the rolls a bit and warm them up. Set 2 eggplant slices in each warm roll.

Grilled Steak With Parsley Salad

Servings:4
Cooking Time: 45 Minutes
Ingredients:
- 1 ½ pounds flatiron steak
- 3 tablespoons olive oil
- Salt and pepper to taste
- 2 cups parsley leaves
- ½ cup parmesan cheese, grated
- 1 tablespoon fresh lemon juice

Directions:
1. Preheat the air fryer at 390°F.
2. Place the grill pan accessory in the air fryer.
3. Mix together the steak, oil, salt and pepper.
4. Grill for 15 minutes per batch and make sure to flip the meat halfway through the cooking time.

5. Meanwhile, prepare the salad by combining in a bowl the parsley leaves, parmesan cheese and lemon juice. Season with salt and pepper.

Inside-out Cheeseburgers

Servings: 3
Cooking Time: 9-11 Minutes
Ingredients:
- 1 pound 2 ounces 90% lean ground beef
- ¾ teaspoon Dried oregano
- ¾ teaspoon Table salt
- ¾ teaspoon Ground black pepper
- ¼ teaspoon Garlic powder
- 6 tablespoons Shredded Cheddar, Swiss, or other semi-firm cheese, or a purchased blend of shredded cheeses
- 3 Hamburger buns (gluten-free, if a concern), split open

Directions:
1. Preheat the air fryer to 375°F .
2. Gently mix the ground beef, oregano, salt, pepper, and garlic powder in a bowl until well combined without turning the mixture to mush. Form it into two 6-inch patties for the small batch, three for the medium, or four for the large.
3. Place 2 tablespoons of the shredded cheese in the center of each patty. With clean hands, fold the sides of the patty up to cover the cheese, then pick it up and roll it gently into a ball to seal the cheese inside. Gently press it back into a 5-inch burger without letting any cheese squish out. Continue filling and preparing more burgers, as needed.
4. Place the burgers in the basket in one layer and air-fry undisturbed for 8 minutes for medium or 10 minutes for well-done.
5. Use a nonstick-safe spatula, and perhaps a flatware fork for balance, to transfer the burgers to a cutting board. Set the buns cut side down in the basket in one layer and air-fry undisturbed for 1 minute, to toast a bit and warm up. Cool the burgers a few minutes more, then serve them warm in the buns.

Oregano And Coconut Scramble

Servings: 4
Cooking Time: 20 Minutes
Ingredients:
- 8 eggs, whisked
- 2 tablespoons oregano, chopped
- Salt and black pepper to the taste
- 2 tablespoons parmesan, grated
- ¼ cup coconut cream

Directions:
1. In a bowl, mix the eggs with all the ingredients and whisk. Pour this into a pan that fits your air fryer, introduce it in the preheated fryer and cook at 350°F for 20 minutes, stirring often. Divide the scramble between plates and serve for breakfast.

Pigs In A Blanket

Servings: 10
Cooking Time: 8 Minutes
Ingredients:
- 1 cup all-purpose flour, plus more for rolling
- 1 teaspoon baking powder
- ¼ cup salted butter, cut into small pieces
- ½ cup buttermilk
- 10 fully cooked breakfast sausage links

Directions:
1. In a large mixing bowl, whisk together the flour and baking powder. Using your fingers or a pastry blender, cut in the butter until you have small pea-size crumbles.
2. Using a rubber spatula, make a well in the center of the flour mixture. Pour the buttermilk into the well, and fold the mixture together until you form a dough ball.
3. Place the sticky dough onto a floured surface and, using a floured rolling pin, roll out until ½-inch thick. Using a round biscuit cutter, cut out 10 rounds, reshaping the dough and rolling out, as needed.
4. Place 1 fully cooked breakfast sausage link on the left edge of each biscuit and roll up, leaving the ends slightly exposed.
5. Using a pastry brush, brush the biscuits with the whisked eggs, and spray them with cooking spray.
6. Place the pigs in a blanket into the air fryer basket with at least 1 inch between each biscuit. Set the air fryer to 340°F and cook for 8 minutes.

Sausage Bacon Fandango

Servings:4
Cooking Time:20 Minutes
Ingredients:
- 8 bacon slices
- 8 chicken sausages
- 4 eggs
- Salt and black pepper, to taste

Directions:
1. Preheat the Air fryer to 320°F and grease 4 ramekins lightly.
2. Place bacon slices and sausages in the Air fryer basket.
3. Cook for about 10 minutes and crack 1 egg in each prepared ramekin.
4. Season with salt and black pepper and cook for about 10 more minutes.
5. Divide bacon slices and sausages in serving plates.
6. Place 1 egg in each plate and serve warm.

Bacon Puff Pastry Pinwheels

Servings: 8
Cooking Time: 10 Minutes
Ingredients:
- 1 sheet of puff pastry
- 2 tablespoons maple syrup
- ¼ cup brown sugar
- 8 slices bacon (not thick cut)
- coarsely cracked black pepper
- vegetable oil

Directions:
1. On a lightly floured surface, roll the puff pastry out into a square that measures roughly 10 inches wide by however long your bacon strips are. Cut the pastry into eight even strips.
2. Brush the strips of pastry with the maple syrup and sprinkle the brown sugar on top, leaving 1 inch of dough exposed at the far end of each strip. Place a slice of bacon on each strip of puff pastry, letting 1/8-inch of the length of bacon hang over the edge of the pastry. Season generously with coarsely ground black pepper.
3. With the exposed end of the pastry strips away from you, roll the bacon and pastry strips up into pinwheels. Dab a little water on the exposed end of the pastry and pinch it to the pinwheel to seal the pastry shut.
4. Preheat the air fryer to 360°F.
5. Brush or spray the air fryer basket with a little vegetable oil. Place the pinwheels into the basket and air-fry at 360°F for 8 minutes. Turn the pinwheels over and air-fry for another 2 minutes to brown the bottom. Serve warm.

English Breakfast

Servings: 2
Cooking Time: 30 Minutes
Ingredients:
- 6 bacon strips
- 1 cup cooked white beans
- 1 tbsp melted butter
- ½ tbsp flour
- Salt and pepper to taste
- 2 eggs

Directions:
1. Preheat air fryer to 360°F. In a second bowl, combine the beans, butter, flour, salt, and pepper. Mix well. Put the bacon in the frying basket and Air Fry for 10 minutes, flipping once. Remove the bacon and stir in the beans. Crack the eggs on top and cook for 10-12 minutes until the eggs are set. Serve with bacon.

Onion Marinated Skirt Steak

Servings:3
Cooking Time: 45 Minutes
Ingredients:
- 1 large red onion, grated or pureed
- 2 tablespoons brown sugar
- 1 tablespoon vinegar
- 1 ½ pounds skirt steak
- Salt and pepper to taste

Directions:
1. Place all ingredients in a Ziploc bag and allow to marinate in the fridge for at least 2 hours.
2. Preheat the air fryer at 390°F.
3. Place the grill pan accessory in the air fryer.
4. Grill for 15 minutes per batch.
5. Flip every 8 minutes for even grilling.

Cheese Pie

Servings: 4
Cooking Time: 16 Minutes
Ingredients:
- 8 eggs
- 1 1/2 cups heavy whipping cream
- 1 lb cheddar cheese, grated
- Pepper
- Salt

Directions:
1. Preheat the air fryer to 325°F.
2. In a bowl, whisk together cheese, eggs, whipping cream, pepper, and salt.
3. Spray air fryer baking dish with cooking spray.

4. Pour egg mixture into the prepared dish and place in the air fryer basket.
5. Cook for 16 minutes or until the egg is set.
6. Serve and enjoy.

Mini Bagels

Servings:6
Cooking Time: 10 Minutes
Ingredients:
- 2 cups blanched finely ground almond flour
- 2 cups shredded mozzarella cheese
- 3 tablespoons salted butter, divided
- 1½ teaspoons baking powder
- 1 teaspoon apple cider vinegar
- 2 large eggs, divided

Directions:
1. In a large microwave-safe bowl, combine flour, mozzarella, and 1 tablespoon butter. Microwave on high 90 seconds, then form into a soft ball of dough.
2. Add baking powder, vinegar, and 1 egg to dough, stirring until fully combined.
3. Once dough is cool enough to work with your hands, about 2 minutes, divide evenly into six balls. Poke a hole in each ball of dough with your finger and gently stretch each ball out to be 2" in diameter.
4. In a small microwave-safe bowl, melt remaining butter in microwave on high 30 seconds, then let cool 1 minute. Whisk with remaining egg, then brush mixture over each bagel.
5. Line air fryer basket with parchment paper and place bagels onto ungreased parchment, working in batches if needed.
6. Adjust the temperature to 350°F and set the timer for 10 minutes. Halfway through, use tongs to flip bagels for even cooking.
7. Allow bagels to set and cool completely, about 15 minutes, before serving. Store leftovers in a sealed bag in the refrigerator up to 4 days.

Strawberry Toast

Servings: 4
Cooking Time: 8 Minutes
Ingredients:
- 4 slices bread, ½-inch thick
- butter-flavored cooking spray
- 1 cup sliced strawberries
- 1 teaspoon sugar

Directions:
1. Spray one side of each bread slice with butter-flavored cooking spray. Lay slices sprayed side down.
2. Divide the strawberries among the bread slices.
3. Sprinkle evenly with the sugar and place in the air fryer basket in a single layer.
4. Cook at 390°F for 8minutes. The bottom should look brown and crisp and the top should look glazed.

Egg Muffins

Servings: 4
Cooking Time: 11 Minutes
Ingredients:
- 4 eggs
- salt and pepper
- olive oil
- 4 English muffins, split
- 1 cup shredded Colby Jack cheese
- 4 slices ham or Canadian bacon

Directions:
1. Preheat air fryer to 390°F.
2. Beat together eggs and add salt and pepper to taste. Spray air fryer baking pan lightly with oil and add eggs. Cook for 2minutes, stir, and continue cooking for 4minutes, stirring every minute, until eggs are scrambled to your preference. Remove pan from air fryer.
3. Place bottom halves of English muffins in air fryer basket. Take half of the shredded cheese and divide it among the muffins. Top each with a slice of ham and one-quarter of the eggs. Sprinkle remaining cheese on top of the eggs. Use a fork to press the cheese into the egg a little so it doesn't slip off before it melts.
4. Cook at 360°F for 1 minute. Add English muffin tops and cook for 4minutes to heat through and toast the muffins.

Scrambled Eggs

Servings: 2
Cooking Time: 6 Minutes
Ingredients:

- 4 eggs
- 1/4 tsp garlic powder
- 1/4 tsp onion powder
- 1 tbsp parmesan cheese
- Pepper
- Salt

Directions:
1. Whisk eggs with garlic powder, onion powder, parmesan cheese, pepper, and salt.
2. Pour egg mixture into the air fryer baking dish.
3. Place dish in the air fryer and cook at 360°F for 2 minutes. Stir quickly and cook for 3-4 minutes more.
4. Stir well and serve.

Not-so-english Muffins

Servings: 4
Cooking Time: 10 Minutes
Ingredients:
- 2 strips turkey bacon, cut in half crosswise
- 2 whole-grain English muffins, split
- 1 cup fresh baby spinach, long stems removed
- ¼ ripe pear, peeled and thinly sliced
- 4 slices Provolone cheese

Directions:
1. Place bacon strips in air fryer basket and cook for 2 minutes. Check and separate strips if necessary so they cook evenly. Cook for 4 more minutes, until crispy. Remove and drain on paper towels.
2. Place split muffin halves in air fryer basket and cook at 390°F for 2 minutes, just until lightly browned.
3. Open air fryer and top each muffin with a quarter of the baby spinach, several pear slices, a strip of bacon, and a slice of cheese.
4. Cook at 360°F for 2 minutes, until cheese completely melts.

Mushrooms Spread

Servings: 4
Cooking Time: 20 Minutes
Ingredients:
- 1 cup white mushrooms
- ¼ cup mozzarella, shredded
- ½ cup coconut cream
- A pinch of salt and black pepper
- Cooking spray

Directions:
1. Put the mushrooms in your air fryer's basket, grease with cooking spray and cook at 370°F for 20 minutes. Transfer to a blender, add the remaining ingredients, pulse well, divide into bowls and serve as a spread.

Parmesan Breakfast Casserole

Servings: 3
Cooking Time: 20 Minutes
Ingredients:

- 5 eggs
- 2 tbsp heavy cream
- 3 tbsp chunky tomato sauce
- 2 tbsp parmesan cheese, grated

Directions:

1. Preheat the air fryer to 325°F.
2. In mixing bowl, combine together cream and eggs.
3. Add cheese and tomato sauce and mix well.
4. Spray air fryer baking dish with cooking spray.
5. Pour mixture into baking dish and place in the air fryer basket.
6. Cook for 20 minutes.
7. Serve and enjoy.

Chicken Saltimbocca Sandwiches

Servings: 3
Cooking Time: 11 Minutes
Ingredients:

- 3 5- to 6-ounce boneless skinless chicken breasts
- 6 Thin prosciutto slices
- 6 Provolone cheese slices
- 3 Long soft rolls, such as hero, hoagie, or Italian sub rolls (gluten-free, if a concern), split open lengthwise
- 3 tablespoons Pesto, purchased or homemade

Directions:

1. Preheat the air fryer to 400°F.
2. Wrap each chicken breast with 2 prosciutto slices, spiraling the prosciutto around the breast and overlapping the slices a bit to cover the breast. The prosciutto will stick to the chicken more readily than bacon does.
3. When the machine is at temperature, set the wrapped chicken breasts in the basket and air-fry undisturbed for 10 minutes, or until the prosciutto is frizzled and the chicken is cooked through.
4. Overlap 2 cheese slices on each breast. Air-fry undisturbed for 1 minute, or until melted. Take the basket out of the machine.
5. Smear the insides of the rolls with the pesto, then use kitchen tongs to put a wrapped and cheesy chicken breast in each roll.

Chives Omelet

Servings: 4
Cooking Time: 20 Minutes
Ingredients:

- 6 eggs, whisked
- 1 cup chives, chopped
- Cooking spray
- 1 cup mozzarella, shredded
- Salt and black pepper to the taste

Directions:

1. In a bowl, mix all the ingredients except the cooking spray and whisk well. Grease a pan that fits your air fryer with the cooking spray, pour the eggs mix, spread, put the pan into the machine and cook at 350°F for 20 minutes. Divide the omelet between plates and serve for breakfast.

English Muffin Sandwiches

Servings: 4
Cooking Time: 15 Minutes
Ingredients:

- 4 English muffins
- 8 pepperoni slices
- 4 cheddar cheese slices
- 1 tomato, sliced

Directions:

1. Preheat air fryer to 370°F. Split open the English muffins along the crease. On the bottom half of the muffin, layer 2 slices of pepperoni and one slice of the cheese and tomato. Place the top half of the English muffin to finish the sandwich. Lightly spray with cooking oil. Place the muffin sandwiches in the air fryer. Bake for 8 minutes, flipping once. Let cool slightly before serving.

Breakfast Chimichangas

Servings: 4
Cooking Time: 8 Minutes
Ingredients:
- Four 8-inch flour tortillas
- ½ cup canned refried beans
- 1 cup scrambled eggs
- ½ cup grated cheddar or Monterey jack cheese
- 1 tablespoon vegetable oil
- 1 cup salsa

Directions:
1. Lay the flour tortillas out flat on a cutting board. In the center of each tortilla, spread 2 tablespoons refried beans. Next, add ¼ cup eggs and 2 tablespoons cheese to each tortilla.
2. To fold the tortillas, begin on the left side and fold to the center. Then fold the right side into the center. Next fold the bottom and top down and roll over to completely seal the chimichanga. Using a pastry brush or oil mister, brush the tops of the tortilla packages with oil.
3. Preheat the air fryer to 400°F for 4 minutes. Place the chimichangas into the air fryer basket, seam side down, and air fry for 4 minutes. Using tongs, turn over the chimichangas and cook for an additional 2 to 3 minutes or until light golden brown.

Hard-"boiled" Eggs

Servings:6
Cooking Time: 15 Minutes
Ingredients:
- 6 large eggs

Directions:
1. Preheat the air fryer to 280°F.
2. Place eggs in the air fryer basket and cook 15 minutes. Store cooked eggs in the refrigerator until ready to use, or peel and serve warm.

Cheese Eggs And Leeks

Servings: 2
Cooking Time: 7 Minutes
Ingredients:
- 2 leeks, chopped
- 4 eggs, whisked
- ¼ cup Cheddar cheese, shredded
- ½ cup Mozzarella cheese, shredded
- 1 teaspoon avocado oil

Directions:
1. Preheat the air fryer to 400°F. Then brush the air fryer basket with avocado oil and combine the eggs with the rest of the ingredients inside. Cook for 7 minutes and serve.

Coconut Eggs Mix

Servings: 4
Cooking Time: 8 Minutes
Ingredients:
- 1 tablespoon olive oil
- 1 and ½ cup coconut cream
- 8 eggs, whisked
- ½ cup mint, chopped
- Salt and black pepper to the taste

Directions:
1. In a bowl, mix the cream with salt, pepper, eggs and mint, whisk, pour into the air fryer greased with the oil, spread, cook at 350°F for 8 minutes, divide between plates and serve.

Almond Oatmeal

Servings: 4
Cooking Time: 15 Minutes
Ingredients:
- 2 cups almond milk
- 1 cup coconut, shredded
- 2 teaspoons stevia
- 2 teaspoons vanilla extract

Directions:
1. In a pan that fits your air fryer, mix all the ingredients, stir well, introduce the pan in the machine and cook at 360°F for 15 minutes. Divide into bowls and serve for breakfast.

Cheesy Bell Pepper Eggs

Servings:4
Cooking Time: 15 Minutes
Ingredients:
- 4 medium green bell peppers, tops removed, seeded
- 1 tablespoon coconut oil
- 3 ounces chopped cooked no-sugar-added ham
- ¼ cup peeled and chopped white onion
- 4 large eggs
- ½ teaspoon salt
- 1 cup shredded mild Cheddar cheese

Directions:
1. Place peppers upright into ungreased air fryer basket. Drizzle each pepper with coconut oil. Divide ham and onion evenly among peppers.
2. In a medium bowl, whisk eggs, then sprinkle with salt. Pour mixture evenly into each pepper. Top each with ¼ cup Cheddar.
3. Adjust the temperature to 320°F and set the timer for 15 minutes. Peppers will be tender and eggs will be firm when done.
4. Serve warm on four medium plates.

Bacon, Egg, And Cheese Calzones

Servings:4

Cooking Time: 12 Minutes

Ingredients:

- 2 large eggs
- 1 cup blanched finely ground almond flour
- 2 cups shredded mozzarella cheese
- 2 ounces cream cheese, softened and broken into small pieces
- 4 slices cooked sugar-free bacon, crumbled

Directions:

1. Beat eggs in a small bowl. Pour into a medium nonstick skillet over medium heat and scramble. Set aside.

2. In a large microwave-safe bowl, mix flour and mozzarella. Add cream cheese to bowl.

3. Place bowl in microwave and cook 45 seconds on high to melt cheese, then stir with a fork until a soft dough ball forms.

4. Cut a piece of parchment to fit air fryer basket. Separate dough into two sections and press each out into an 8" round.

5. On half of each dough round, place half of the scrambled eggs and crumbled bacon. Fold the other side of the dough over and press to seal the edges.

6. Place calzones on ungreased parchment and into air fryer basket. Adjust the temperature to 350°F and set the timer for 12 minutes, turning calzones halfway through cooking. Crust will be golden and firm when done.

7. Let calzones cool on a cooking rack 5 minutes before serving.

Bacon & Hot Dogs Omelet

Servings:2

Cooking Time: 10 Minutes

Ingredients:

- 4 eggs
- 1 bacon slice, chopped
- 2 hot dogs, chopped
- 2 small onions, chopped

Directions:

1. Set the temperature of Air Fryer to 320°F.

2. In an Air Fryer baking pan, crack the eggs and beat them well.

3. Now, add in the remaining ingredients and gently, stir to combine.

4. Air Fry for about 10 minutes.

5. Serve hot.

Coconut Pudding

Servings: 4

Cooking Time: 20 Minutes

Ingredients:

- 1 cup cauliflower rice
- ½ cup coconut, shredded
- 3 cups coconut milk
- 2 tablespoons stevia

Directions:

1. In a pan that fits the air fryer, combine all the ingredients and whisk well. Introduce the in your air fryer and cook at 360°F for 20 minutes. Divide into bowls and serve for breakfast.

Mediterranean Egg Sandwich

Servings: 1

Cooking Time: 8 Minutes

Ingredients:

- 1 large egg
- 5 baby spinach leaves, chopped
- 1 tablespoon roasted bell pepper, chopped
- 1 English muffin
- 1 thin slice prosciutto or Canadian bacon

Directions:

1. Spray a ramekin with cooking spray or brush the inside with extra-virgin olive oil.

2. In a small bowl, whisk together the egg, baby spinach, and bell pepper.

3. Split the English muffin in half and spray the inside lightly with cooking spray or brush with extra-virgin olive oil.

4. Preheat the air fryer to 350°F for 2 minutes. Place the egg ramekin and open English muffin into the air fryer basket, and cook at 350°F for 5 minutes. Open the air fryer drawer and add the prosciutto or bacon; cook for an additional 1 minute.

5. To assemble the sandwich, place the egg on one half of the English muffin, top with prosciutto or bacon, and place the remaining piece of English muffin on top.

Smoked Salmon Croissant Sandwich

Servings: 1
Cooking Time: 30 Minutes
Ingredients:
- 1 croissant, halved
- 2 eggs
- 1 tbsp guacamole
- 1 smoked salmon slice
- Salt and pepper to taste

Directions:
1. Preheat air fryer to 360°F. Place the croissant, crusty side up, in the frying basket side by side. Whisk the eggs in a small ceramic dish until fluffy. Place in the air fryer. Bake for 10 minutes. Gently scramble the half-cooked egg in the baking dish with a fork. Flip the croissant and cook for another 10 minutes until the scrambled eggs are cooked, but still fluffy, and the croissant is toasted.

2. Place one croissant on a serving plate, then spread the guacamole on top. Scoop the scrambled eggs onto guacamole, then top with smoked salmon. Sprinkle with salt and pepper. Top with the second slice of toasted croissant, close sandwich, and serve hot.

Scotch Eggs

Servings:6
Cooking Time: 15 Minutes
Ingredients:
- 1 pound ground pork breakfast sausage
- 6 large hard-boiled eggs, peeled
- 1 cup all-purpose flour
- 2 large eggs, beaten
- 2 cups plain bread crumbs

Directions:
1. Preheat the air fryer to 375°F.
2. Separate sausage into six equal amounts and flatten into patties.
3. Form sausage patties around hard-boiled eggs, completely enclosing them.
4. In three separate small bowls, place flour, eggs, and bread crumbs.
5. Roll each sausage-covered egg first in flour, then egg, and finally bread crumbs. Place rolled eggs in the air fryer basket and spritz them with cooking spray.
6. Cook 15 minutes, turning halfway through cooking time and spraying any dry spots with additional cooking spray. Serve warm.

Grilled Bbq Sausages

Servings:3
Cooking Time: 30 Minutes
Ingredients:
- 6 sausage links
- ½ cup prepared BBQ sauce

Directions:
1. Preheat the air fryer at 390°F.
2. Place the grill pan accessory in the air fryer.
3. Place the sausage links and grill for 30 minutes.
4. Flip halfway through the cooking time.
5. Before serving brush with prepared BBQ sauce.

Goat Cheese, Beet, And Kale Frittata

Servings: 6
Cooking Time: 20 Minutes
Ingredients:
- 6 large eggs
- ½ teaspoon garlic powder
- ¼ teaspoon black pepper
- ¼ teaspoon salt
- 1 cup chopped kale
- 1 cup cooked and chopped red beets
- ⅓ cup crumbled goat cheese

Directions:
1. Preheat the air fryer to 320°F.
2. In a medium bowl, whisk the eggs with the garlic powder, pepper, and salt. Mix in the kale, beets, and goat cheese.
3. Spray an oven-safe 7-inch springform pan with cooking spray. Pour the egg mixture into the pan and place it in the air fryer basket.
4. Cook for 20 minutes, or until the internal temperature reaches 145°F.
5. When the frittata is cooked, let it set for 5 minutes before removing from the pan.
6. Slice and serve immediately.

Chocolate Chip Scones

Servings:8
Cooking Time:15 Minutes
Ingredients:
- ½ cup cold salted butter, divided
- 2 cups all-purpose flour
- ½ cup brown sugar
- ½ teaspoon baking powder
- 1 large egg
- ¾ cup buttermilk
- ½ cup semisweet chocolate chips

Directions:
1. Preheat the air fryer to 320°F. Cut parchment paper to fit the air fryer basket.
2. Chill 6 tablespoons butter in the freezer 10 minutes. In a small microwave-safe bowl, microwave remaining 2 tablespoons butter 30 seconds until melted, and set aside.
3. In a large bowl, mix flour, brown sugar, and baking powder.
4. Remove butter from freezer and grate into bowl. Use a wooden spoon to evenly distribute.
5. Add egg and buttermilk and stir gently until a soft, sticky dough forms. Gently fold in chocolate chips.
6. Turn dough out onto a lightly floured surface. Fold a couple of times and gently form into a 6" round. Cut into eight triangles.
7. Place scones on parchment in the air fryer basket, leaving at least 2" space between each, working in batches as necessary.
8. Brush each scone with melted butter. Cook 15 minutes until scones are dark golden brown and crispy on the edges, and a toothpick inserted into the center comes out clean. Serve warm.

Baked Eggs

Servings: 4
Cooking Time: 6 Minutes
Ingredients:
- 4 large eggs
- ⅛ teaspoon black pepper
- ⅛ teaspoon salt

Directions:
1. Preheat the air fryer to 330°F. Place 4 silicone muffin liners into the air fryer basket.
2. Crack 1 egg at a time into each silicone muffin liner. Sprinkle with black pepper and salt.
3. Bake for 6 minutes. Remove and let cool 2 minutes prior to serving.

Appetizers And Snacks Recipes

Cheese Rounds

Servings:4
Cooking Time: 6 Minutes
Ingredients:
- 1 cup Cheddar cheese, shredded

Directions:
1. Preheat the air fryer to 400°F. Then line the air fryer basket with baking paper. Sprinkle the cheese on the baking paper in the shape of small rounds. Cook them for 6 minutes or until the cheese is melted and starts to be crispy.

Root Vegetable Crisps

Servings: 4
Cooking Time: 8 Minutes
Ingredients:
- 1 small taro root, peeled and washed
- 1 small yucca root, peeled and washed
- 1 small purple sweet potato, washed
- 2 cups filtered water
- 2 teaspoons extra-virgin olive oil
- ½ teaspoon salt

Directions:
1. Using a mandolin, slice the taro root, yucca root, and purple sweet potato into ⅛-inch slices.
2. Add the water to a large bowl. Add the sliced vegetables and soak for at least 30 minutes.
3. Preheat the air fryer to 370°F.
4. Drain the water and pat the vegetables dry with a paper towel or kitchen cloth. Toss the vegetables with the olive oil and sprinkle with salt. Liberally spray the air fryer basket with olive oil mist.
5. Place the vegetables into the air fryer basket, making sure not to overlap the pieces.
6. Cook for 8 minutes, shaking the basket every 2 minutes, until the outer edges start to turn up and the vegetables start to brown. Remove from the basket and serve warm. Repeat with the remaining vegetable slices until all are cooked.

Sweet And Spicy Beef Jerky

Servings:6
Cooking Time: 4 Hours
Ingredients:
- 1 pound eye of round beef, fat trimmed, sliced into ¼"-thick strips
- ¼ cup soy sauce
- 2 tablespoons sriracha hot chili sauce
- ½ teaspoon ground black pepper
- 2 tablespoons granular brown erythritol

Directions:
1. Place beef in a large sealable bowl or bag. Pour soy sauce and sriracha into bowl or bag, then sprinkle in pepper and erythritol. Shake or stir to combine ingredients and coat steak. Cover and place in refrigerator to marinate at least 2 hours up to overnight.
2. Once marinated, remove strips from marinade and pat dry. Place into ungreased air fryer basket in a single layer, working in batches if needed. Adjust the temperature to 180°F and set the timer for 4 hours. Jerky will be chewy and dark brown when done. Store in airtight container in a cool, dry place up to 2 weeks.

Croutons

Servings:4
Cooking Time: 5 Minutes
Ingredients:
- 4 slices sourdough bread, diced into small cubes
- 2 tablespoons salted butter, melted
- 1 teaspoon chopped fresh parsley
- 2 tablespoons grated Parmesan cheese

Directions:
1. Preheat the air fryer to 400°F.
2. Place bread cubes in a large bowl.
3. Pour butter over bread cubes. Add parsley and Parmesan. Toss bread cubes until evenly coated.
4. Place bread cubes in the air fryer basket in a single layer. Cook 5 minutes until well toasted. Serve cooled for maximum crunch.

Crispy Curried Sweet Potato Fries

Servings: 4
Cooking Time: 20 Minutes
Ingredients:
- ½ cup sour cream
- ½ cup peach chutney
- 3 tsp curry powder
- 2 sweet potatoes, julienned
- 1 tbsp olive oil
- Salt and pepper to taste

Directions:
1. Preheat air fryer to 390°F. Mix together sour cream, peach chutney, and 1 ½ tsp curry powder in a small bowl. Set aside. In a medium bowl, add sweet potatoes, olive oil, the rest of the curry powder, salt, and pepper. Toss to coat. Place the potatoes in the frying basket. Bake for about 6 minutes, then shake the basket once. Cook for an additional 4 -6 minutes or until the potatoes are golden and crispy. Serve the fries hot in a basket along with the chutney sauce for dipping.

Sweet-and-salty Pretzels

Servings: 4
Cooking Time: 5 Minutes
Ingredients:
- 2 cups Plain pretzel nuggets
- 1 tablespoon Worcestershire sauce
- 2 teaspoons Granulated white sugar
- 1 teaspoon Mild smoked paprika
- ½ teaspoon Garlic or onion powder

Directions:
1. Preheat the air fryer to 350°F .
2. Put the pretzel nuggets, Worcestershire sauce, sugar, smoked paprika, and garlic or onion powder in a large bowl. Toss gently until the nuggets are well coated.
3. When the machine is at temperature, pour the nuggets into the basket, spreading them into as close to a single layer as possible. Air-fry, shaking the basket three or four times to rearrange the nuggets, for 5 minutes, or until the nuggets are toasted and aromatic. Although the coating will darken, don't let it burn, especially if the machine's temperature is 360°F.
4. Pour the nuggets onto a wire rack and gently spread them into one layer. Cool for 5 minutes before serving.

Crispy Salami Roll-ups

Servings:16
Cooking Time: 4 Minutes
Ingredients:
- 4 ounces cream cheese, broken into 16 equal pieces
- 16 deli slices Genoa salami

Directions:
1. Place a piece of cream cheese at the edge of a slice of salami and roll to close. Secure with a toothpick. Repeat with remaining cream cheese pieces and salami.
2. Place roll-ups in an ungreased 6" round nonstick baking dish and place into air fryer basket. Adjust the temperature to 350°F and set the timer for 4 minutes. Salami will be crispy and cream cheese will be warm when done. Let cool 5 minutes before serving.

Cauliflower Buns

Servings:8
Cooking Time: 12 Minutes
Ingredients:
- 1 steamer bag cauliflower, cooked according to package instructions
- ½ cup shredded mozzarella cheese
- ¼ cup shredded mild Cheddar cheese
- ¼ cup blanched finely ground almond flour
- 1 large egg
- ½ teaspoon salt

Directions:
1. Let cooked cauliflower cool about 10 minutes. Use a kitchen towel to wring out excess moisture, then place cauliflower in a food processor.
2. Add mozzarella, Cheddar, flour, egg, and salt to the food processor and pulse twenty times until mixture is combined. It will resemble a soft, wet dough.
3. Divide mixture into eight piles. Wet your hands with water to prevent sticking, then press each pile into a flat bun shape, about ½" thick.
4. Cut a sheet of parchment to fit air fryer basket. Working in batches if needed, place the formed dough onto ungreased parchment in air fryer basket. Adjust the temperature to 350°F and set the timer for 12 minutes, turning buns halfway through cooking.
5. Let buns cool 10 minutes before serving. Serve warm.

Bacon-wrapped Jalapeño Poppers

Servings:4
Cooking Time: 12 Minutes

Ingredients:
- 3 ounces full-fat cream cheese
- ½ cup shredded sharp Cheddar cheese
- ¼ teaspoon garlic powder
- 6 jalapeño peppers, trimmed and halved lengthwise, seeded and membranes removed
- 12 slices bacon

Directions:
1. Preheat the air fryer to 400°F.
2. In a large microwave-safe bowl, place cream cheese, Cheddar, and garlic powder. Microwave 20 seconds until softened and stir. Spoon cheese mixture into hollow jalapeño halves.
3. Wrap a bacon slice around each jalapeño half, completely covering pepper.
4. Place in the air fryer basket and cook 12 minutes, turning halfway through cooking time. Serve warm.

Halloumi Fries

Servings: 3
Cooking Time: 12 Minutes
Ingredients:
- 1½ tablespoons Olive oil
- 1½ teaspoons Minced garlic
- ⅛ teaspoon Dried oregano
- ⅛ teaspoon Dried thyme
- ⅛ teaspoon Table salt
- ⅛ teaspoon Ground black pepper
- ¾ pound Halloumi

Directions:
1. Preheat the air fryer to 400°F.
2. Whisk the oil, garlic, oregano, thyme, salt, and pepper in a medium bowl.
3. Lay the piece of halloumi flat on a cutting board. Slice it widthwise into ½-inch-thick sticks. Cut each stick lengthwise into ½-inch-thick batons.
4. Put these batons into the olive oil mixture. Toss gently but well to coat.
5. Place the batons in the basket in a single layer. Air-fry undisturbed for 12 minutes, or until lightly browned, particularly at the edges.
6. Dump the fries out onto a wire rack. They may need a little coaxing with a nonstick-safe spatula to come free. Cool for a couple of minutes before serving hot.

Home-style Taro Chips

Servings: 2
Cooking Time: 20 Minutes
Ingredients:
- 1 tbsp olive oil
- 1 cup thinly sliced taro
- Salt to taste
- ½ cup hummus

Directions:
1. Preheat air fryer to 325°F. Put the sliced taro in the greased frying basket, spread the pieces out, and drizzle with olive oil. Air Fry for 10-12 minutes, shaking the basket twice. Sprinkle with salt and serve with hummus.

Thyme Sweet Potato Chips

Servings: 2
Cooking Time: 20 Minutes
Ingredients:
- 1 tbsp olive oil
- 1 sweet potato, sliced
- ¼ tsp dried thyme
- Salt to taste

Directions:
1. Preheat air fryer to 390°F. Spread the sweet potato slices in the greased basket and brush with olive oil. Air Fry for 6 minutes. Remove the basket, shake, and sprinkle with thyme and salt. Cook for 6 more minutes or until lightly browned. Serve warm and enjoy!

Bacon-wrapped Goat Cheese Poppers

Servings: 10
Cooking Time: 10 Minutes
Ingredients:
- 10 large jalapeño peppers
- 8 ounces goat cheese
- 10 slices bacon

Directions:
1. Preheat the air fryer to 380°F.
2. Slice the jalapeños in half. Carefully remove the veins and seeds of the jalapeños with a spoon.
3. Fill each jalapeño half with 2 teaspoons goat cheese.
4. Cut the bacon in half lengthwise to make long strips. Wrap the jalapeños with bacon, trying to cover the entire length of the jalapeño.
5. Place the bacon-wrapped jalapeños into the air fryer basket. Cook the stuffed jalapeños for 10 minutes or until bacon is crispy.

Beet Chips

Servings: 4
Cooking Time: 20 Minutes
Ingredients:
- 2 large red beets, washed and skinned
- 1 tablespoon avocado oil
- ¼ teaspoon salt

Directions:
1. Preheat the air fryer to 330°F.
2. Using a mandolin or sharp knife, slice the beets in ⅛-inch slices. Place them in a bowl of water and let them soak for 30 minutes. Drain the water and pat the beets dry with a paper towel or kitchen cloth.
3. In a medium bowl, toss the beets with avocado oil and sprinkle them with salt.
4. Lightly spray the air fryer basket with olive oil mist and place the beet chips into the basket. To allow for even cooking, don't overlap the beets; cook in batches if necessary.
5. Cook the beet chips 15 to 20 minutes, shaking the basket every 5 minutes, until the outer edges of the beets begin to flip up like a chip. Remove from the basket and serve warm. Repeat with the remaining chips until they're all cooked.

Plantain Chips

Servings: 2
Cooking Time: 14 Minutes
Ingredients:
- 1 large green plantain
- 2½ cups filtered water, divided
- 2 teaspoons sea salt, divided
- Cooking spray

Directions:
1. Slice the plantain into 1-inch pieces. Place the plantains into a large bowl, cover with 2 cups water and 1 teaspoon salt. Soak the plantains for 30 minutes; then remove and pat dry.
2. Preheat the air fryer to 390°F.
3. Place the plantain pieces into the air fryer basket, leaving space between the plantain rounds. Cook the plantains for 5 minutes, and carefully remove them from the air fryer basket.
4. Add the remaining water to a small bowl.
5. Using a small drinking glass, dip the bottom of the glass into the water and mash the warm plantains until they're ¼-inch thick. Return the plantains to the air fryer basket, sprinkle with the remaining sea salt, and spray lightly with cooking spray.
6. Cook for another 6 to 8 minutes, or until lightly golden brown edges appear.

Bacon Candy

Servings: 6
Cooking Time: 6 Minutes
Ingredients:
- 1½ tablespoons Honey
- 1 teaspoon White wine vinegar
- 3 Extra thick–cut bacon strips, halved widthwise (gluten-free, if a concern)
- ½ teaspoon Ground black pepper

Directions:
1. Preheat the air fryer to 350°F .
2. Whisk the honey and vinegar in a small bowl until incorporated.
3. When the machine is at temperature, remove the basket. Lay the bacon strip halves in the basket in one layer. Brush the tops with the honey mixture; sprinkle each bacon strip evenly with black pepper.
4. Return the basket to the machine and air-fry undisturbed for 6 minutes, or until the bacon is crunchy. Or a little less time if you prefer bacon that's still pliable, an extra minute if you want the bacon super crunchy. Take care that the honey coating doesn't burn. Remove the basket from the machine and set aside for 5 minutes. Use kitchen tongs to transfer the bacon strips to a serving plate.

Mini Greek Meatballs

Servings:36
Cooking Time: 10 Minutes
Ingredients:
- 1 cup fresh spinach leaves
- ¼ cup peeled and diced red onion
- ½ cup crumbled feta cheese
- 1 pound 85/15 ground turkey
- ½ teaspoon salt
- ½ teaspoon ground cumin
- ¼ teaspoon ground black pepper

Directions:
1. Place spinach, onion, and feta in a food processor, and pulse ten times until spinach is chopped. Scoop into a large bowl.
2. Add turkey to bowl and sprinkle with salt, cumin, and pepper. Mix until fully combined. Roll mixture into thirty-six meatballs.
3. Place meatballs into ungreased air fryer basket, working in batches if needed. Adjust the temperature to 350°F and set the timer for 10 minutes, shaking basket twice during cooking. Meatballs will be browned and have an internal temperature of at least 165°F when done. Serve warm.

Bacon-wrapped Mozzarella Sticks

Servings:6
Cooking Time: 12 Minutes
Ingredients:
- 6 sticks mozzarella string cheese
- 6 slices sugar-free bacon

Directions:
1. Place mozzarella sticks on a medium plate, cover, and place into freezer 1 hour until frozen solid.
2. Wrap each mozzarella stick in 1 piece of bacon and secure with a toothpick. Place into ungreased air fryer basket. Adjust the temperature to 400°F and set the timer for 12 minutes, turning sticks once during cooking. Bacon will be crispy when done. Serve warm.

Sweet Apple Fries

Servings: 3
Cooking Time: 8 Minutes
Ingredients:
- 2 Medium-size sweet apple(s), such as Gala or Fuji
- 1 Large egg white(s)
- 2 tablespoons Water
- 1½ cups Finely ground gingersnap crumbs (gluten-free, if a concern)
- Vegetable oil spray

Directions:
1. Preheat the air fryer to 375°F .
2. Peel and core an apple, then cut it into 12 slices. Repeat with more apples as necessary.
3. Whisk the egg white(s) and water in a medium bowl until foamy. Add the apple slices and toss well to coat.
4. Spread the gingersnap crumbs across a dinner plate. Using clean hands, pick up an apple slice, let any excess egg white mixture slip back into the rest, and dredge the slice in the crumbs, coating it lightly but evenly on all sides. Set it aside and continue coating the remaining apple slices.
5. Lightly coat the slices on all sides with vegetable oil spray, then set them curved side down in the basket in one layer. Air-fry undisturbed for 6 minutes, or until browned and crisp. You may need to air-fry the slices for 2 minutes longer if the temperature is at 360°F.
6. Use kitchen tongs to transfer the slices to a wire rack. Cool for 2 to 3 minutes before serving.

Curly's Cauliflower

Servings: 4

Cooking Time: 30 Minutes

Ingredients:

- 4 cups bite-sized cauliflower florets
- 1 cup friendly bread crumbs, mixed with 1 tsp. salt
- ¼ cup melted butter [vegan/other]
- ¼ cup buffalo sauce [vegan/other]
- Mayo [vegan/other] or creamy dressing for dipping

Directions:

1. In a bowl, combine the butter and buffalo sauce to create a creamy paste.

2. Completely cover each floret with the sauce.

3. Coat the florets with the bread crumb mixture. Cook the florets in the Air Fryer for approximately 15 minutes at 350°F, shaking the basket occasionally.

4. Serve with a raw vegetable salad, mayo or creamy dressing.

Roasted Peanuts

Servings:10

Cooking Time: 14 Minutes

Ingredients:

- 2½ cups raw peanuts
- 1 tablespoon olive oil
- Salt, as required

Directions:

1. Set the temperature of Air Fryer to 320°F.

2. Add the peanuts in an Air Fryer basket in a single layer.

3. Air Fry for about 9 minutes, tossing twice.

4. Remove the peanuts from Air Fryer basket and transfer into a bowl.

5. Add the oil, and salt and toss to coat well.

6. Return the nuts mixture into Air Fryer basket.

7. Air Fry for about 5 minutes.

8. Once done, transfer the hot nuts in a glass or steel bowl and serve.

Pepperoni Chips

Servings:2

Cooking Time: 8 Minutes

Ingredients:

- 14 slices pepperoni

Directions:

1. Place pepperoni slices into ungreased air fryer basket. Adjust the temperature to 350°F and set the timer for 8 minutes. Pepperoni will be browned and crispy when done. Let cool 5 minutes before serving.

Store in airtight container at room temperature up to 3 days.

Crispy Ravioli Bites

Servings: 5

Cooking Time: 7 Minutes

Ingredients:

- ⅓ cup All-purpose flour
- 1 Large egg(s), well beaten
- ⅔ cup Seasoned Italian-style dried bread crumbs
- 10 ounces Frozen mini ravioli, meat or cheese, thawed
- Olive oil spray

Directions:

1. Preheat the air fryer to 400°F.

2. Pour the flour into a medium bowl. Set up and fill two shallow soup plates or small pie plates on your counter: one with the beaten egg(s) and one with the bread crumbs.

3. Pour all the ravioli into the flour and toss well to coat. Pick up 1 ravioli, gently shake off any excess flour, and dip the ravioli in the egg(s), coating both sides. Let any excess egg slip back into the rest, then set the ravioli in the bread crumbs, turning it several times until lightly and evenly coated on all sides. Set aside on a cutting board and continue on with the remaining ravioli.

4. Lightly coat the ravioli on both sides with olive oil spray, then set them in the basket in as close to a single layer as you can. Some can lean up against the side of the basket. Air-fry for 7 minutes, tossing the basket at the 4-minute mark to rearrange the pieces, until brown and crisp.

5. Pour the contents of the basket onto a wire rack. Cool for 5 minutes before serving.

Broccoli Florets

Servings: 4

Cooking Time: 20 Minutes

Ingredients:

- 1 lb. broccoli, cut into florets
- 1 tbsp. lemon juice
- 1 tbsp. olive oil
- 1 tbsp. sesame seeds
- 3 garlic cloves, minced

Directions:

1. In a bowl, combine all of the ingredients, coating the broccoli well.

2. Transfer to the Air Fryer basket and air fry at 400°F for 13 minutes.

Buffalo Bites

Servings: 16
Cooking Time: 12 Minutes
Ingredients:
- 1 pound ground chicken
- 8 tablespoons buffalo wing sauce
- 2 ounces Gruyère cheese, cut into 16 cubes
- 1 tablespoon maple syrup

Directions:
1. Mix 4 tablespoons buffalo wing sauce into all the ground chicken.
2. Shape chicken into a log and divide into 16 equal portions.
3. With slightly damp hands, mold each chicken portion around a cube of cheese and shape into a firm ball. When you have shaped 8 meatballs, place them in air fryer basket.
4. Cook at 390°F for approximately 5minutes. Shake basket, reduce temperature to 360°F, and cook for 5 minutes longer.
5. While the first batch is cooking, shape remaining chicken and cheese into 8 more meatballs.
6. Repeat step 4 to cook second batch of meatballs.
7. In a medium bowl, mix the remaining 4 tablespoons of buffalo wing sauce with the maple syrup. Add all the cooked meatballs and toss to coat.
8. Place meatballs back into air fryer basket and cook at 390°F for 2 minutes to set the glaze. Skewer each with a toothpick and serve.

Classic Potato Chips

Servings: 4
Cooking Time: 8 Minutes
Ingredients:
- 2 medium russet potatoes, washed
- 2 cups filtered water
- 1 tablespoon avocado oil
- ½ teaspoon salt

Directions:
1. Using a mandolin, slice the potatoes into ⅛-inch-thick pieces.
2. Pour the water into a large bowl. Place the potatoes in the bowl and soak for at least 30 minutes.
3. Preheat the air fryer to 350°F.
4. Drain the water and pat the potatoes dry with a paper towel or kitchen cloth. Toss with avocado oil and salt. Liberally spray the air fryer basket with olive oil mist.
5. Set the potatoes inside the air fryer basket, separating them so they're not on top of each other. Cook for 5 minutes, shake the basket, and cook another 5 minutes, or until browned.
6. Remove and let cool a few minutes prior to serving. Repeat until all the chips are cooked.

Korean-style Wings

Servings: 4
Cooking Time: 10 Minutes
Ingredients:
- 1 pound chicken wings, drums and flats separated
- ½ teaspoon salt
- ¼ teaspoon ground black pepper
- ¼ cup gochujang sauce
- 2 tablespoons soy sauce
- 1 teaspoon ground ginger
- ¼ cup mayonnaise

Directions:
1. Preheat the air fryer to 350°F.
2. Sprinkle wings with salt and pepper. Place wings in the air fryer basket and cook 15 minutes, turning halfway through cooking time.
3. In a medium bowl, mix gochujang sauce, soy sauce, ginger, and mayonnaise.
4. Toss wings in sauce mixture and adjust the air fryer temperature to 400°F.
5. Place wings back in the air fryer basket and cook an additional 5 minutes until the internal temperature reaches at least 165°F. Serve warm.

Onion Ring Nachos

Servings: 3
Cooking Time: 8 Minutes
Ingredients:
- ¾ pound Frozen breaded (not battered) onion rings (do not thaw)
- 1½ cups Shredded Cheddar, Monterey Jack, or Swiss cheese, or a purchased Tex-Mex blend
- Up to 12 Pickled jalapeño rings

Directions:
1. Preheat the air fryer to 400°F.
2. When the machine is at temperature, spread the onion rings in the basket in a fairly even layer. Air-fry undisturbed for 6 minutes, or until crisp. Remove the basket from the machine.
3. Cut a circle of parchment paper to line a 6-inch round cake pan for a small air fryer, a 7-inch round cake pan for a medium air fryer, or an 8-inch round cake pan for a large machine.
4. Pour the onion rings into a fairly even layer in the cake pan, then sprinkle the cheese evenly over them. Dot with the jalapeño rings.
5. Set the pan in the basket and air-fry undisturbed for 2 minutes, until the cheese has melted and is bubbling.
6. Remove the pan from the basket. Cool for 5 minutes before serving.

Apple Rollups

Servings: 8

Cooking Time: 5 Minutes

Ingredients:

- 8 slices whole wheat sandwich bread
- 4 ounces Colby Jack cheese, grated
- ½ small apple, chopped
- 2 tablespoons butter, melted

Directions:

1. Remove crusts from bread and flatten the slices with rolling pin. Don't be gentle. Press hard so that bread will be very thin.
2. Top bread slices with cheese and chopped apple, dividing the ingredients evenly.
3. Roll up each slice tightly and secure each with one or two toothpicks.
4. Brush outside of rolls with melted butter.
5. Place in air fryer basket and cook at 390°F for 5minutes, until outside is crisp and nicely browned.

Bacon Butter

Servings:5

Cooking Time: 2 Minutes

Ingredients:

- ½ cup butter
- 3 oz bacon, chopped

Directions:

1. Preheat the air fryer to 400°F and put the bacon inside. Cook it for 8 minutes. Stir the bacon every 2 minutes. Meanwhile, soften the butter in the oven and put it in the butter mold. Add cooked bacon and churn the butter. Refrigerate the butter for 30 minutes.

Buttered Corn On The Cob

Servings:2

Cooking Time:20 Minutes

Ingredients:

- 2 corn on the cob
- 2 tablespoons butter, softened and divided
- Salt and black pepper, to taste

Directions:

1. Preheat the Air fryer to 320°F and grease an Air fryer basket.
2. Season the cobs evenly with salt and black pepper and rub with 1 tablespoon butter.
3. Wrap the cobs in foil paper and arrange in the Air fryer basket.
4. Cook for about 20 minutes and top with remaining butter.
5. Dish out and serve warm.

Bacon & Blue Cheese Tartlets

Servings: 6

Cooking Time: 30 Minutes

Ingredients:

- 6 bacon slices
- 16 phyllo tartlet shells
- ½ cup diced blue cheese
- 3 tbsp apple jelly

Directions:

1. Preheat the air fryer to 400°F. Put the bacon in a single layer in the frying basket and Air Fry for 14 minutes, turning once halfway through. Remove and drain on paper towels, then crumble when cool. Wipe the fryer clean. Fill the tartlet shells with bacon and the blue cheese cubes and add a dab of apple jelly on top of the filling. Lower the temperature to 350°F, then put the shells in the frying basket. Air Fry until the cheese melts and the shells brown, about 5-6 minutes. Remove and serve.

Parmesan Zucchini Fries

Servings:8

Cooking Time: 10 Minutes

Ingredients:

- 2 medium zucchini, ends removed, quartered lengthwise, and sliced into 3"-long fries
- ½ teaspoon salt
- ⅓ cup heavy whipping cream
- ½ cup blanched finely ground almond flour
- ¾ cup grated Parmesan cheese
- 1 teaspoon Italian seasoning

Directions:

1. Sprinkle zucchini with salt and wrap in a kitchen towel to draw out excess moisture. Let sit 2 hours.
2. Pour cream into a medium bowl. In a separate medium bowl, whisk together flour, Parmesan, and Italian seasoning.
3. Place each zucchini fry into cream, then gently shake off excess. Press each fry into dry mixture, coating each side, then place into ungreased air fryer basket. Adjust the temperature to 400°F and set the timer for 10 minutes, turning fries halfway through cooking. Fries will be golden and crispy when done. Place on clean parchment sheet to cool 5 minutes before serving.

Avocado Fries

Servings: 4
Cooking Time: 20 Minutes
Ingredients:
- ½ cup panko
- ½ tsp. salt
- 1 whole avocado
- 1 oz. aquafaba

Directions:
1. In a shallow bowl, stir together the panko and salt.
2. In a separate shallow bowl, add the aquafaba.
3. Dip the avocado slices into the aquafaba, before coating each one in the panko.
4. Place the slices in your Air Fryer basket, taking care not to overlap any. Air fry for 10 minutes at 390°F.

Skinny Fries

Servings: 2
Cooking Time: 15 Minutes
Ingredients:
- 2 to 3 russet potatoes, peeled and cut into ¼-inch sticks
- 2 to 3 teaspoons olive or vegetable oil
- salt

Directions:
1. Cut the potatoes into ¼-inch strips. Rinse the potatoes with cold water several times and let them soak in cold water for at least 10 minutes or as long as overnight.
2. Preheat the air fryer to 380°F.
3. Drain and dry the potato sticks really well, using a clean kitchen towel. Toss the fries with the oil in a bowl and then air-fry the fries in two batches at 380°F for 15 minutes, shaking the basket a couple of times while they cook.
4. Add the first batch of French fries back into the air fryer basket with the finishing batch and let everything warm through for a few minutes. As soon as the fries are done, season them with salt and transfer to a plate or basket. Serve them warm with ketchup or your favorite dip.

Crispy Spiced Chickpeas

Servings: 2
Cooking Time: 20 Minutes
Ingredients:
- 1 can chickpeas, drained
- ½ teaspoon salt
- ½ teaspoon chili powder
- ¼ teaspoon ground cinnamon
- ⅛ teaspoon smoked paprika
- pinch ground cayenne pepper
- 1 tablespoon olive oil

Directions:
1. Preheat the air fryer to 400°F.
2. Dry the chickpeas as well as you can with a clean kitchen towel, rubbing off any loose skins as necessary. Combine the spices in a small bowl. Toss the chickpeas with the olive oil and then add the spices and toss again.
3. Air-fry for 15 minutes, shaking the basket a couple of times while they cook.
4. Check the chickpeas to see if they are crispy enough and if necessary, air-fry for another 5 minutes to crisp them further. Serve warm, or cool to room temperature and store in an airtight container for up to two weeks.

Parmesan Crackers

Servings: 6
Cooking Time: 6 Minutes
Ingredients:
- 2 cups finely grated Parmesan cheese
- ¼ teaspoon paprika
- ¼ teaspoon garlic powder
- ½ teaspoon dried thyme
- 1 tablespoon all-purpose flour

Directions:
1. Preheat the air fryer to 380°F.
2. In a medium bowl, stir together the Parmesan, paprika, garlic powder, thyme, and flour.
3. Line the air fryer basket with parchment paper.
4. Using a tablespoon measuring tool, create 1-tablespoon mounds of seasoned cheese on the parchment paper, leaving 2 inches between the mounds to allow for spreading.
5. Cook the crackers for 6 minutes. Allow the cheese to harden and cool before handling. Repeat in batches with the remaining cheese.

Roasted Carrots

Servings: 2
Cooking Time: 20 Minutes
Ingredients:
- 1 tbsp. olive oil
- 3 cups baby carrots or carrots, cut into large chunks
- 1 tbsp. honey
- Salt and pepper to taste

Directions:
1. In a bowl, coat the carrots with the honey and olive oil before sprinkling on some salt and pepper.
2. Place into the Air Fryer and cook at 390°F for 12 minutes. Serve hot.

Bacon-y Cauliflower Skewers

Servings:4
Cooking Time: 12 Minutes
Ingredients:
- 4 slices sugar-free bacon, cut into thirds
- ¼ medium yellow onion, peeled and cut into 1" pieces
- 4 ounces cauliflower florets
- 1½ tablespoons olive oil
- ¼ teaspoon salt
- ¼ teaspoon garlic powder

Directions:
1. Place 1 piece bacon and 2 pieces onion on a 6" skewer. Add a second piece bacon, and 2 cauliflower florets, followed by another piece of bacon onto skewer. Repeat with remaining ingredients and three additional skewers to make four total skewers.
2. Drizzle skewers with olive oil, then sprinkle with salt and garlic powder. Place skewers into ungreased air fryer basket. Adjust the temperature to 375°F and set the timer for 12 minutes, turning the skewers halfway through cooking. When done, vegetables will be tender and bacon will be crispy. Serve warm.

Cauliflower "tater" Tots

Servings: 6
Cooking Time: 10 Minutes
Ingredients:
- 1 head of cauliflower
- 2 eggs
- ¼ cup all-purpose flour*
- ½ cup grated Parmesan cheese
- 1 teaspoon salt
- freshly ground black pepper
- vegetable or olive oil, in a spray bottle

Directions:
1. Grate the head of cauliflower with a box grater or finely chop it in a food processor. You should have about 3½ cups. Place the chopped cauliflower in the center of a clean kitchen towel and twist the towel tightly to squeeze all the water out of the cauliflower.
2. Place the squeezed cauliflower in a large bowl. Add the eggs, flour, Parmesan cheese, salt and freshly ground black pepper. Shape the cauliflower into small cylinders or "tater tot" shapes, rolling roughly one tablespoon of the mixture at a time. Place the tots on a cookie sheet lined with paper towel to absorb any residual moisture. Spray the cauliflower tots all over with oil.
3. Preheat the air fryer to 400°F.
4. Air-fry the tots at 400°F, one layer at a time for 10 minutes, turning them over for the last few minutes of the cooking process for even browning. Season with salt and black pepper. Serve hot with your favorite dipping sauce.

Fried Mozzarella Sticks

Servings: 7
Cooking Time: 5 Minutes
Ingredients:
- 7 1-ounce string cheese sticks, unwrapped
- ½ cup All-purpose flour or tapioca flour
- 2 Large egg(s), well beaten
- 2¼ cups Seasoned Italian-style dried bread crumbs (gluten-free, if a concern)
- Olive oil spray

Directions:
1. Unwrap the string cheese and place the pieces in the freezer for 20 minutes.
2. Preheat the air fryer to 400°F.
3. Set up and fill three shallow soup plates or small pie plates on your counter: one for the flour, one for the egg(s), and one for the bread crumbs.
4. Dip a piece of cold string cheese in the flour until well coated. Gently tap off any excess flour, then set the stick in the egg(s). Roll it around to coat, let any excess egg mixture slip back into the rest, and set the stick in the bread crumbs. Gently roll it around to coat it evenly, even the ends. Now dip it back in the egg(s), then again in the bread crumbs, rolling it to coat well and evenly. Set the stick aside on a cutting board and coat the remaining pieces of string cheese in the same way.
5. Lightly coat the sticks all over with olive oil spray. Place them in the basket in one layer and air-fry undisturbed for 5 minutes, or until golden brown and crisp.
6. Remove the basket from the machine and cool for 5 minutes. Use a nonstick-safe spatula to transfer the mozzarella sticks to a serving platter. Serve hot.

Tomato & Garlic Roasted Potatoes

Servings: 4
Cooking Time: 25 Minutes
Ingredients:
- 16 cherry tomatoes, halved
- 6 red potatoes, cubed
- 3 garlic cloves, minced
- Salt and pepper to taste
- 1 tsp chopped chives
- 1 tbsp extra-virgin olive oil

Directions:
1. Preheat air fryer to 370°F. Combine cherry potatoes, garlic, salt, pepper, chives and olive oil in a resealable plastic bag. Seal and shake the bag. Put the potatoes in the greased frying basket and Roast for 10 minutes. Shake the basket, place the cherry tomatoes in, and cook for 10 more minutes. Allow to cool slightly and serve.

Rumaki

Servings: 24
Cooking Time: 12 Minutes
Ingredients:
- 10 ounces raw chicken livers
- 1 can sliced water chestnuts, drained
- ¼ cup low-sodium teriyaki sauce
- 12 slices turkey bacon
- toothpicks

Directions:
1. Cut livers into 1½-inch pieces, trimming out tough veins as you slice.
2. Place livers, water chestnuts, and teriyaki sauce in small container with lid. If needed, add another tablespoon of teriyaki sauce to make sure livers are covered. Refrigerate for 1 hour.
3. When ready to cook, cut bacon slices in half crosswise.
4. Wrap 1 piece of liver and 1 slice of water chestnut in each bacon strip. Secure with toothpick.
5. When you have wrapped half of the livers, place them in the air fryer basket in a single layer.
6. Cook at 390°F for 12 minutes, until liver is done and bacon is crispy.
7. While first batch cooks, wrap the remaining livers. Repeat step 6 to cook your second batch.

Spicy Cheese-stuffed Mushrooms

Servings:20
Cooking Time: 8 Minutes
Ingredients:
- 4 ounces cream cheese, softened
- 6 tablespoons shredded pepper jack cheese
- 2 tablespoons chopped pickled jalapeños
- 20 medium button mushrooms, stems removed
- 2 tablespoons olive oil
- ¼ teaspoon salt
- ⅛ teaspoon ground black pepper

Directions:
1. In a large bowl, mix cream cheese, pepper jack, and jalapeños together.
2. Drizzle mushrooms with olive oil, then sprinkle with salt and pepper. Spoon 2 tablespoons cheese mixture into each mushroom and place in a single layer into ungreased air fryer basket. Adjust the temperature to 370°F and set the timer for 8 minutes, checking halfway through cooking to ensure even cooking, rearranging if some are darker than others. When they're golden and cheese is bubbling, mushrooms will be done. Serve warm.

Thick-crust Pepperoni Pizza

Servings: 2
Cooking Time: 10 Minutes
Ingredients:
- 10 ounces Purchased fresh pizza dough (not a prebaked crust)
- Olive oil spray
- ¼ cup Purchased pizza sauce
- 10 slices Sliced pepperoni
- ⅓ cup Purchased shredded Italian 3- or 4-cheese blend

Directions:
1. Preheat the air fryer to 400°F.
2. Generously coat the inside of a 6-inch round cake pan for a small air fryer, a 7-inch round cake pan for a medium air fryer, or an 8-inch round cake pan for a large model with olive oil spray.
3. Set the dough in the pan and press it to fill the bottom in an even, thick layer. Spread the sauce over the dough, then top with the pepperoni and cheese.
4. When the machine is at temperature, set the pan in the basket and air-fry undisturbed for 10 minutes, or until puffed, brown, and bubbling.
5. Use kitchen tongs to transfer the cake pan to a wire rack. Cool for only a minute or so. Use a spatula to loosen the pizza from the pan and lift it out and onto the rack. Continue cooling for a few minutes before cutting into wedges to serve.

Asian Five-spice Wings

Servings: 4
Cooking Time: 15 Minutes
Ingredients:
- 2 pounds chicken wings
- ½ cup Asian-style salad dressing
- 2 tablespoons Chinese five-spice powder

Directions:
1. Cut off wing tips and discard or freeze for stock. Cut remaining wing pieces in two at the joint.
2. Place wing pieces in a large sealable plastic bag. Pour in the Asian dressing, seal bag, and massage the marinade into the wings until well coated. Refrigerate for at least an hour.
3. Remove wings from bag, drain off excess marinade, and place wings in air fryer basket.
4. Cook at 360°F for 15minutes or until juices run clear. About halfway through cooking time, shake the basket or stir wings for more even cooking.
5. Transfer cooked wings to plate in a single layer. Sprinkle half of the Chinese five-spice powder on the wings, turn, and sprinkle other side with remaining seasoning.

Zucchini Chips

Servings: 3
Cooking Time: 17 Minutes
Ingredients:
- 1½ small Zucchini, washed but not peeled, and cut into ¼-inch-thick rounds
- Olive oil spray
- ¼ teaspoon Table salt

Directions:
1. Preheat the air fryer to 375°F.
2. Lay some paper towels on your work surface. Set the zucchini rounds on top, then set more paper towels over the rounds. Press gently to remove some of the moisture. Remove the top layer of paper towels and lightly coat the rounds with olive oil spray on both sides.
3. When the machine is at temperature, set the rounds in the basket, overlapping them a bit as needed. Air-fry for 15 minutes, tossing and rearranging the rounds at the 5- and 10-minute marks, until browned, soft, yet crisp at the edges.
4. Gently pour the contents of the basket onto a wire rack. Cool for at least 10 minutes or up to 2 hours before serving.

Garlic–cream Cheese Wontons

Servings: 4
Cooking Time: 8 Minutes
Ingredients:
- 6 ounces full-fat cream cheese, softened
- 1 teaspoon garlic powder
- 12 wonton wrappers
- ¼ cup water

Directions:
1. Preheat the air fryer to 375°F.
2. In a medium bowl, mix cream cheese and garlic powder until smooth.
3. For each wonton, place 1 tablespoon cream cheese mixture in center of a wonton wrapper.
4. Brush edges of wonton with water to help it seal. Fold wonton to form a triangle. Spritz both sides with cooking spray. Repeat with remaining wontons and cream cheese mixture.
5. Place wontons in the air fryer basket. Cook 8 minutes, turning halfway through cooking time, until golden brown and crispy. Serve warm.

Bacon-wrapped Cabbage Bites

Servings:6
Cooking Time: 12 Minutes
Ingredients:
- 3 tablespoons sriracha hot chili sauce, divided
- 1 medium head cabbage, cored and cut into 12 bite-sized pieces
- 2 tablespoons coconut oil, melted
- ½ teaspoon salt
- 12 slices sugar-free bacon
- ½ cup mayonnaise
- ¼ teaspoon garlic powder

Directions:
1. Evenly brush 2 tablespoons sriracha onto cabbage pieces. Drizzle evenly with coconut oil, then sprinkle with salt.
2. Wrap each cabbage piece with bacon and secure with a toothpick. Place into ungreased air fryer basket. Adjust the temperature to 375°F and set the timer for 12 minutes, turning cabbage halfway through cooking. Bacon will be cooked and crispy when done.
3. In a small bowl, whisk together mayonnaise, garlic powder, and remaining sriracha. Use as a dipping sauce for cabbage bites.

Beef Taco–stuffed Meatballs

Servings:6
Cooking Time: 15 Minutes
Ingredients:
- 4 ounces Colby jack cheese cut into ½" cubes
- 1 pound 80/20 ground beef
- 1 packet taco seasoning
- ½ cup bread crumbs

Directions:
1. Preheat the air fryer to 350°F. Chill cheese in the freezer 15 minutes.

2. In a large bowl, mix beef, taco seasoning, and bread crumbs. Roll mixture into balls, about 2" each, to make eighteen meatballs.

3. Remove cheese from freezer. Place one cube into each meatball by pressing gently into the center and shaping meat around cheese. Roll into a ball.

4. Spritz meatballs with cooking spray and place in the air fryer basket. Cook 15 minutes, shaking the basket three times during cooking, until meatballs are brown and internal temperature has reached at least 165°F. Serve warm.

Vegetarians Recipes

Garlicky Roasted Mushrooms

Servings: 4
Cooking Time: 30 Minutes
Ingredients:
- 16 garlic cloves, peeled
- 2 tsp olive oil
- 16 button mushrooms
- 2 tbsp fresh chives, snipped
- Salt and pepper to taste
- 1 tbsp white wine

Directions:
1. Preheat air fryer to 350°F. Coat the garlic with some olive oil in a baking pan, then Roast in the air fryer for 12 minutes. When done, take the pan out and stir in the mushrooms, salt, and pepper. Then add the remaining olive oil and white wine. Put the pan back into the fryer and Bake for 10-15 minutes until the mushrooms and garlic soften. Sprinkle with chives and serve warm.

Crispy Shawarma Broccoli

Servings: 4
Cooking Time: 25 Minutes
Ingredients:
- 1 pound broccoli, steamed and drained
- 2 tablespoons canola oil
- 1 teaspoon cayenne pepper
- 1 teaspoon sea salt
- 1 tablespoon Shawarma spice blend

Directions:
1. Toss all ingredients in a mixing bowl.

2. Roast in the preheated Air Fryer at 380°F for 10 minutes, shaking the basket halfway through the cooking time.

3. Work in batches. Bon appétit!

Cheesy Brussel Sprouts

Servings:3
Cooking Time:10 Minutes
Ingredients:
- 1 pound Brussels sprouts, trimmed and halved
- ¼ cup whole wheat breadcrumbs
- ¼ cup Parmesan cheese, shredded
- 1 tablespoon balsamic vinegar
- 1 tablespoon extra-virgin olive oil
- Salt and black pepper, to taste

Directions:
1. Preheat the Air fryer to 400°F and grease an Air fryer basket.

2. Mix Brussel sprouts, vinegar, oil, salt, and black pepper in a bowl and toss to coat well.

3. Arrange the Brussel sprouts in the Air fryer basket and cook for about 5 minutes.

4. Sprinkle with breadcrumbs and cheese and cook for about 5 more minutes.

5. Dish out and serve hot.

Vegetable Burgers

Servings:4
Cooking Time: 12 Minutes
Ingredients:

- 8 ounces cremini mushrooms
- 2 large egg yolks
- ½ medium zucchini, trimmed and chopped
- ¼ cup peeled and chopped yellow onion
- 1 clove garlic, peeled and finely minced
- ½ teaspoon salt
- ¼ teaspoon ground black pepper

Directions:

1. Place all ingredients into a food processor and pulse twenty times until finely chopped and combined.
2. Separate mixture into four equal sections and press each into a burger shape. Place burgers into ungreased air fryer basket. Adjust the temperature to 375°F and set the timer for 12 minutes, turning burgers halfway through cooking. Burgers will be browned and firm when done.
3. Place burgers on a large plate and let cool 5 minutes before serving.

Broccoli & Parmesan Dish

Servings:4
Cooking Time: 25 Minutes
Ingredients:

- 1 tbsp olive oil
- 1 lemon, Juiced
- Salt and pepper to taste
- 1-ounce Parmesan cheese, grated

Directions:

1. In a bowl, mix all ingredients. Add the mixture to your air fryer and cook for 20 minutes at 360°F. Serve.

Colorful Vegetable Medley

Servings: 4
Cooking Time: 20 Minutes
Ingredients:

- 1 lb green beans, chopped
- 2 carrots, cubed
- Salt and pepper to taste
- 1 zucchini, cut into chunks
- 1 red bell pepper, sliced
- Cooking spray

Directions:

1. Preheat air fryer to 390°F. Combine green beans, carrots, salt and pepper in a large bowl. Spray with cooking oil and transfer to the frying basket. Roast for 6 minutes.
2. Combine zucchini and red pepper in a bowl. Season to taste and spray with cooking oil; set aside. When the cooking time is up, add the zucchini and red pepper to the basket. Cook for another 6 minutes. Serve and enjoy.

Gourmet Wasabi Popcorn

Servings: 2
Cooking Time: 30 Minutes
Ingredients:

- 1/2 teaspoon brown sugar
- 1 teaspoon salt
- 1/2 teaspoon wasabi powder, sifted
- 1 tablespoon avocado oil
- 3 tablespoons popcorn kernels

Directions:

1. Add the dried corn kernels to the Air Fryer basket; toss with the remaining ingredients.
2. Cook at 395°F for 15 minutes, shaking the basket every 5 minutes. Work in two batches.
3. Taste, adjust the seasonings and serve immediately. Bon appétit!

Tacos

Servings: 24
Cooking Time: 8 Minutes Per Batch
Ingredients:

- 1 24-count package 4-inch corn tortillas
- 1½ cups refried beans
- 4 ounces sharp Cheddar cheese, grated
- ½ cup salsa
- oil for misting or cooking spray

Directions:

1. Preheat air fryer to 390°F.
2. Wrap refrigerated tortillas in damp paper towels and microwave for 30 to 60 seconds to warm. If necessary, rewarm tortillas as you go to keep them soft enough to fold without breaking.
3. Working with one tortilla at a time, top with 1 tablespoon of beans, 1 tablespoon of grated cheese, and 1 teaspoon of salsa. Fold over and press down very gently on the center. Press edges firmly all around to seal. Spray both sides with oil or cooking spray.
4. Cooking in two batches, place half the tacos in the air fryer basket. To cook 12 at a time, you may need to stand them upright and lean some against the sides of basket. It's okay if they're crowded as long as you leave a little room for air to circulate around them.
5. Cook for 8 minutes or until golden brown and crispy.
6. Repeat steps 4 and 5 to cook remaining tacos.

Cinnamon Sugar Tortilla Chips

Servings: 4
Cooking Time: 20 Minutes
Ingredients:
- 4 flour tortillas
- 1/4 cup vegan margarine, melted
- 1 ½ tablespoons ground cinnamon
- 1/4 cup caster sugar

Directions:
1. Slice each tortilla into eight slices. Brush the tortilla pieces with the melted margarine.
2. In a mixing bowl, thoroughly combine the cinnamon and sugar. Toss the cinnamon mixture with the tortillas.
3. Transfer to the cooking basket and cook at 360°F for 8 minutes or until lightly golden. Work in batches.
4. They will crisp up as they cool. Serve and enjoy!

Sweet And Sour Brussel Sprouts

Servings:2
Cooking Time:10 Minutes
Ingredients:
- 2 cups Brussels sprouts, trimmed and halved lengthwise
- 1 tablespoon balsamic vinegar
- 1 tablespoon maple syrup
- Salt, as required

Directions:
1. Preheat the Air fryer to 400°F and grease an Air fryer basket.
2. Mix all the ingredients in a bowl and toss to coat well.
3. Arrange the Brussel sprouts in the Air fryer basket and cook for about 10 minutes, shaking once halfway through.
4. Dish out in a bowl and serve hot.

Roasted Vegetable Pita Pizza

Servings: 4
Cooking Time: 20 Minutes
Ingredients:
- 1 medium red bell pepper, seeded and cut into quarters
- 1 teaspoon extra-virgin olive oil
- ⅛ teaspoon black pepper
- ⅛ teaspoon salt
- Two 6-inch whole-grain pita breads
- 6 tablespoons pesto sauce
- ¼ small red onion, thinly sliced
- ½ cup shredded part-skim mozzarella cheese

Directions:
1. Preheat the air fryer to 400°F.
2. In a small bowl, toss the bell peppers with the olive oil, pepper, and salt.
3. Place the bell peppers in the air fryer and cook for 15 minutes, shaking every 5 minutes to prevent burning.
4. Remove the peppers and set aside. Turn the air fryer temperature down to 350°F.
5. Lay the pita bread on a flat surface. Cover each with half the pesto sauce; then top with even portions of the red bell peppers and onions. Sprinkle cheese over the top. Spray the air fryer basket with olive oil mist.
6. Carefully lift the pita bread into the air fryer basket with a spatula.
7. Cook for 5 to 8 minutes, or until the outer edges begin to brown and the cheese is melted.
8. Serve warm with desired sides.

Cheesy Broccoli Sticks

Servings:2
Cooking Time: 16 Minutes
Ingredients:
- 1 steamer bag broccoli florets, cooked according to package instructions
- 1 large egg
- 1 ounce Parmesan 100% cheese crisps, finely ground
- ½ cup shredded sharp Cheddar cheese
- ½ teaspoon salt
- ½ cup ranch dressing

Directions:
1. Let cooked broccoli cool 5 minutes, then place into a food processor with egg, cheese crisps, Cheddar, and salt. Process on low for 30 seconds until all ingredients are combined and begin to stick together.
2. Cut a sheet of parchment paper to fit air fryer basket. Take one scoop of mixture, about 3 tablespoons, and roll into a 4" stick shape, pressing down gently to flatten the top. Place stick on ungreased parchment into air fryer basket. Repeat with remaining mixture to form eight sticks.
3. Adjust the temperature to 350°F and set the timer for 16 minutes, turning sticks halfway through cooking. Sticks will be golden brown when done.
4. Serve warm with ranch dressing on the side for dipping.

Sweet Pepper Nachos

Servings:2
Cooking Time: 5 Minutes
Ingredients:
- 6 mini sweet peppers, seeded and sliced in half
- ¾ cup shredded Colby jack cheese
- ¼ cup sliced pickled jalapeños
- ½ medium avocado, peeled, pitted, and diced
- 2 tablespoons sour cream

Directions:
1. Place peppers into an ungreased 6" round nonstick baking dish. Sprinkle with Colby and top with jalapeños.
2. Place dish into air fryer basket. Adjust the temperature to 350°F and set the timer for 5 minutes. Cheese will be melted and bubbly when done.
3. Remove dish from air fryer and top with avocado. Drizzle with sour cream. Serve warm.

Portobello Mini Pizzas

Servings:4
Cooking Time: 10 Minutes
Ingredients:
- 4 large portobello mushrooms, stems removed
- 2 cups shredded mozzarella cheese, divided
- ½ cup full-fat ricotta cheese
- 1 teaspoon salt, divided
- ½ teaspoon ground black pepper
- 1 teaspoon Italian seasoning
- 1 cup pizza sauce

Directions:
1. Preheat the air fryer to 350°F.
2. Use a spoon to hollow out mushroom caps. Spritz mushrooms with cooking spray. Place ¼ cup mozzarella into each mushroom cap.
3. In a small bowl, mix ricotta, ½ teaspoon salt, pepper, and Italian seasoning. Divide mixture evenly and spoon into mushroom caps.
4. Pour ¼ cup pizza sauce into each mushroom cap, then top each with ¼ cup mozzarella. Sprinkle tops of pizzas with remaining salt.
5. Place mushrooms in the air fryer basket and cook 10 minutes until cheese is brown and bubbling. Serve warm.

Roasted Spaghetti Squash

Servings:6
Cooking Time: 45 Minutes
Ingredients:
- 1 spaghetti squash, halved and seeded
- 2 tablespoons coconut oil
- 4 tablespoons salted butter, melted
- 1 teaspoon garlic powder
- 2 teaspoons dried parsley

Directions:
1. Brush shell of spaghetti squash with coconut oil. Brush inside with butter. Sprinkle inside with garlic powder and parsley.
2. Place squash skin side down into ungreased air fryer basket, working in batches if needed. Adjust the temperature to 350°F and set the timer for 30 minutes. When the timer beeps, flip squash and cook an additional 15 minutes until fork-tender.
3. Use a fork to remove spaghetti strands from shell and serve warm.

Lemony Green Beans

Servings:3
Cooking Time:12 Minutes
Ingredients:
- 1 pound green beans, trimmed and halved
- 1 teaspoon butter, melted
- 1 tablespoon fresh lemon juice
- ¼ teaspoon garlic powder

Directions:
1. Preheat the Air fryer to 400°F and grease an Air fryer basket.
2. Mix all the ingredients in a bowl and toss to coat well.
3. Arrange the green beans into the Air fryer basket and cook for about 12 minutes.
4. Dish out in a serving plate and serve hot.

Almond Flour Battered Wings

Servings:4
Cooking Time: 25 Minutes
Ingredients:
- ¼ cup butter, melted
- ¾ cup almond flour
- 16 pieces chicken wings
- 2 tablespoons stevia powder
- 4 tablespoons minced garlic
- Salt and pepper to taste

Directions:
1. Preheat the air fryer for 5 minutes.
2. In a mixing bowl, combine the chicken wings, almond flour, stevia powder, and garlic Season with salt and pepper to taste.
3. Place in the air fryer basket and cook for 25 minutes at 400°F.
4. Halfway through the cooking time, make sure that you give the fryer basket a shake.
5. Once cooked, place in a bowl and drizzle with melted butter. Toss to coat.

Almond Asparagus

Servings:3
Cooking Time:6 Minutes
Ingredients:
- 1 pound asparagus
- 1/3 cup almonds, sliced
- 2 tablespoons olive oil
- 2 tablespoons balsamic vinegar
- Salt and black pepper, to taste

Directions:
1. Preheat the Air fryer to 400°F and grease an Air fryer basket.
2. Mix asparagus, oil, vinegar, salt, and black pepper in a bowl and toss to coat well.
3. Arrange asparagus into the Air fryer basket and sprinkle with the almond slices.
4. Cook for about 6 minutes and dish out to serve hot.

Zucchini Gratin

Servings: 2
Cooking Time: 15 Minutes
Ingredients:
- 5 oz. parmesan cheese, shredded
- 1 tbsp. coconut flour
- 1 tbsp. dried parsley
- 2 zucchinis
- 1 tsp. butter, melted

Directions:
1. Mix the parmesan and coconut flour together in a bowl, seasoning with parsley to taste.
2. Cut the zucchini in half lengthwise and chop the halves into four slices.
3. Pre-heat the fryer at 400°F.
4. Pour the melted butter over the zucchini and then dip the zucchini into the parmesan-flour mixture, coating it all over. Cook the zucchini in the fryer for thirteen minutes.

Caprese Eggplant Stacks

Servings:4
Cooking Time: 8 Minutes
Ingredients:
- 1 medium eggplant, cut into 4 (½") slices
- ½ teaspoon salt
- ¼ teaspoon ground black pepper
- 4 (¼") slices tomato
- 2 ounces fresh mozzarella cheese, cut into 4 slices
- 1 tablespoon olive oil
- ¼ cup fresh basil, sliced

Directions:
1. Preheat the air fryer to 320°F.
2. In a 6" round pan, place eggplant slices. Sprinkle with salt and pepper. Top each with a tomato slice, then a mozzarella slice, and drizzle with oil.
3. Place in the air fryer basket and cook 8 minutes until eggplant is tender and cheese is melted. Garnish with fresh basil to serve.

Cool Mini Zucchini's

Servings:4
Cooking Time: 25 Minutes
Ingredients:
- 4 large eggs, beaten
- 1 medium zucchini, sliced
- 4 ounces feta cheese, drained and crumbled
- 2 tbsp fresh dill, chopped
- Cooking spray
- Salt and pepper as needed

Directions:
1. Preheat the air fryer to 360°F, and un a bowl, add the beaten eggs and season with salt and pepper.
2. Stir in zucchini, dill and feta cheese. Grease 8 muffin tins with cooking spray. Roll pastry and arrange them to cover the sides of the muffin tins. Divide the egg mixture evenly between the holes. Place the prepared tins in your air fryer and cook for 15 minutes. Serve and enjoy!

Stuffed Mushrooms

Servings:4
Cooking Time: 10 Minutes
Ingredients:
- 12 baby bella mushrooms, stems removed
- 4 ounces full-fat cream cheese, softened
- ¼ cup grated vegetarian Parmesan cheese
- ¼ cup Italian bread crumbs
- 1 teaspoon crushed red pepper flakes

Directions:
1. Preheat the air fryer to 400°F.
2. Use a spoon to hollow out mushroom caps.
3. In a medium bowl, combine cream cheese, Parmesan, bread crumbs, and red pepper flakes. Scoop approximately 1 tablespoon mixture into each mushroom cap.
4. Place stuffed mushrooms in the air fryer basket and cook 10 minutes until stuffing is brown. Let cool 5 minutes before serving.

Twice-baked Broccoli-cheddar Potatoes

Servings:4

Cooking Time: 35 Minutes

Ingredients:

- 4 large russet potatoes
- 2 tablespoons plus 2 teaspoons ranch dressing
- 1 teaspoon salt
- ½ teaspoon ground black pepper
- ¼ cup chopped cooked broccoli florets
- 1 cup shredded sharp Cheddar cheese

Directions:

1. Preheat the air fryer to 400°F.

2. Using a fork, poke several holes in potatoes. Place in the air fryer basket and cook 30 minutes until fork-tender.

3. Once potatoes are cool enough to handle, slice lengthwise and scoop out the cooked potato into a large bowl, being careful to maintain the structural integrity of potato skins. Add ranch dressing, salt, pepper, broccoli, and Cheddar to potato flesh and stir until well combined.

4. Scoop potato mixture back into potato skins and return to the air fryer basket. Cook an additional 5 minutes until cheese is melted. Serve warm.

Crispy Wings With Lemony Old Bay Spice

Servings:4

Cooking Time: 25 Minutes

Ingredients:

- ½ cup butter
- ¾ cup almond flour
- 1 tablespoon old bay spices
- 1 teaspoon lemon juice, freshly squeezed
- 3 pounds chicken wings
- Salt and pepper to taste

Directions:

1. Preheat the air fryer for 5 minutes.

2. In a mixing bowl, combine all ingredients except for the butter.

3. Place in the air fryer basket.

4. Cook for 25 minutes at 350°F.

5. Halfway through the cooking time, shake the fryer basket for even cooking.

6. Once cooked, drizzle with melted butter.

Mediterranean Pan Pizza

Servings:2

Cooking Time: 8 Minutes

Ingredients:

- 1 cup shredded mozzarella cheese
- ¼ medium red bell pepper, seeded and chopped
- ½ cup chopped fresh spinach leaves
- 2 tablespoons chopped black olives
- 2 tablespoons crumbled feta cheese

Directions:

1. Sprinkle mozzarella into an ungreased 6" round nonstick baking dish in an even layer. Add remaining ingredients on top.

2. Place dish into air fryer basket. Adjust the temperature to 350°F and set the timer for 8 minutes, checking halfway through to avoid burning. Top of pizza will be golden brown and the cheese melted when done.

3. Remove dish from fryer and let cool 5 minutes before slicing and serving.

Crustless Spinach And Cheese Frittata

Servings:4

Cooking Time: 20 Minutes

Ingredients:

- 6 large eggs
- ½ cup heavy whipping cream
- 1 cup frozen chopped spinach, drained
- 1 cup shredded sharp Cheddar cheese
- ¼ cup peeled and diced yellow onion
- ½ teaspoon salt
- ¼ teaspoon ground black pepper

Directions:

1. In a large bowl, whisk eggs and cream together. Whisk in spinach, Cheddar, onion, salt, and pepper.

2. Pour mixture into an ungreased 6" round nonstick baking dish. Place dish into air fryer basket. Adjust the temperature to 320°F and set the timer for 20 minutes. Eggs will be firm and slightly browned when done. Serve immediately.

Layered Ravioli Bake

Servings:4

Cooking Time: 20 Minutes

Ingredients:
- 2 cups marinara sauce, divided
- 2 packages fresh cheese ravioli
- 12 slices provolone cheese
- ½ cup Italian bread crumbs
- ½ cup grated vegetarian Parmesan cheese

Directions:
1. Preheat the air fryer to 350°F.
2. In the bottom of a 3-quart baking pan, spread ⅓ cup marinara. Place 6 ravioli on top of the sauce, then add 3 slices provolone on top, then another layer of ⅓ cup marinara. Repeat these layers three times to use up remaining ravioli, provolone, and sauce.
3. In a small bowl, mix bread crumbs and Parmesan. Sprinkle over the top of dish.
4. Cover pan with foil, being sure to tuck foil under the bottom of the pan to ensure the air fryer fan does not blow it off. Place pan in the air fryer basket and cook 15 minutes.
5. Remove foil and cook an additional 5 minutes until the top is brown and bubbling. Serve warm.

Zucchini Fritters

Servings:4

Cooking Time: 12 Minutes

Ingredients:
- 1½ medium zucchini, trimmed and grated
- ½ teaspoon salt, divided
- 1 large egg, whisked
- ¼ teaspoon garlic powder
- ¼ cup grated Parmesan cheese

Directions:
1. Place grated zucchini on a kitchen towel and sprinkle with ¼ teaspoon salt. Wrap in towel and let sit 30 minutes, then wring out as much excess moisture as possible.
2. Place zucchini into a large bowl and mix with egg, remaining salt, garlic powder, and Parmesan. Cut a piece of parchment to fit air fryer basket. Divide mixture into four mounds, about ⅓ cup each, and press out into 4" rounds on ungreased parchment.
3. Place parchment with rounds into air fryer basket. Adjust the temperature to 400°F and set the timer for 12 minutes, turning fritters halfway through cooking. Fritters will be crispy on the edges and tender but firm in the center when done. Serve warm.

Spinach And Feta Pinwheels

Servings:4

Cooking Time: 15 Minutes

Ingredients:
- 1 sheet frozen puff pastry, thawed
- 3 ounces full-fat cream cheese, softened
- 1 bag frozen spinach, thawed and drained
- ¼ teaspoon salt
- ⅓ cup crumbled feta cheese
- 1 large egg, whisked

Directions:
1. Preheat the air fryer to 320°F. Unroll puff pastry into a flat rectangle.
2. In a medium bowl, mix cream cheese, spinach, and salt until well combined.
3. Spoon cream cheese mixture onto pastry in an even layer, leaving a ½" border around the edges.
4. Sprinkle feta evenly across dough and gently press into filling to secure. Roll lengthwise to form a log shape.
5. Cut the roll into twelve 1" pieces. Brush with egg. Place in the air fryer basket and cook 15 minutes, turning halfway through cooking time.
6. Let cool 5 minutes before serving.

Pepper-pineapple With Butter-sugar Glaze

Servings:2

Cooking Time: 10 Minutes

Ingredients:
- 1 medium-sized pineapple, peeled and sliced
- 1 red bell pepper, seeded and julienned
- 1 teaspoon brown sugar
- 2 teaspoons melted butter
- Salt to taste

Directions:
1. Preheat the air fryer to 390°F.
2. Place the grill pan accessory in the air fryer.
3. Mix all ingredients in a Ziploc bag and give a good shake.
4. Dump onto the grill pan and cook for 10 minutes making sure that you flip the pineapples every 5 minutes.

Caramelized Brussels Sprout

Servings:4
Cooking Time:35 Minutes
Ingredients:
- 1 pound Brussels sprouts, trimmed and halved
- 4 teaspoons butter, melted
- Salt and black pepper, to taste

Directions:
1. Preheat the Air fryer to 400°F and grease an Air fryer basket.
2. Mix all the ingredients in a bowl and toss to coat well.
3. Arrange the Brussels sprouts in the Air fryer basket and cook for about 35 minutes.
4. Dish out and serve warm.

Zucchini Topped With Coconut Cream 'n Bacon

Servings:3
Cooking Time: 20 Minutes
Ingredients:
- 1 tablespoon lemon juice
- 3 slices bacon, fried and crumbled
- 3 tablespoons olive oil
- 3 zucchini squashes
- 4 tablespoons coconut cream
- Salt and pepper to taste

Directions:
1. Preheat the air fryer for 5 minutes.
2. Line up chopsticks on both sides of the zucchini and slice thinly until you hit the stick. Brush the zucchinis with olive oil. Set aside.
3. Place the zucchini in the air fryer. Bake for 20 minutes at 350°F.
4. Meanwhile, combine the coconut cream and lemon juice in a mixing bowl. Season with salt and pepper to taste.
5. Once the zucchini is cooked, scoop the coconut cream mixture and drizzle on top.
6. Sprinkle with bacon bits.

Cauliflower Pizza Crust

Servings:2
Cooking Time: 7 Minutes
Ingredients:
- 1 steamer bag cauliflower, cooked according to package instructions
- ½ cup shredded sharp Cheddar cheese
- 1 large egg
- 2 tablespoons blanched finely ground almond flour
- 1 teaspoon Italian seasoning

Directions:
1. Let cooked cauliflower cool for 10 minutes. Using a kitchen towel, wring out excess moisture from cauliflower and place into food processor.
2. Add Cheddar, egg, flour, and Italian seasoning to processor and pulse ten times until cauliflower is smooth and all ingredients are combined.
3. Cut two pieces of parchment paper to fit air fryer basket. Divide cauliflower mixture into two equal portions and press each into a 6" round on ungreased parchment.
4. Place crusts on parchment into air fryer basket. Adjust the temperature to 360°F and set the timer for 7 minutes, gently turning crusts halfway through cooking.
5. Store crusts in refrigerator in an airtight container up to 4 days or freeze between sheets of parchment in a sealable storage bag for up to 2 months.

Wine Infused Mushrooms

Servings:6
Cooking Time: 32 Minutes
Ingredients:
- 1 tablespoon butter
- 2 teaspoons Herbs de Provence
- ½ teaspoon garlic powder
- 2 pounds fresh mushrooms, quartered
- 2 tablespoons white vermouth

Directions:
1. Set the temperature of air fryer to 320°F.
2. In an air fryer pan, mix together the butter, Herbs de Provence, and garlic powder and air fry for about 2 minutes.
3. Stir in the mushrooms and air fry for about 25 minutes.
4. Stir in the vermouth and air fry for 5 more minutes.
5. Remove from air fryer and transfer the mushrooms onto serving plates.
6. Serve hot.

Broccoli Salad

Servings: 2
Cooking Time: 15 Minutes
Ingredients:
- 3 cups fresh broccoli florets
- 2 tbsp. coconut oil, melted
- ¼ cup sliced s
- ½ medium lemon, juiced

Directions:
1. Take a six-inch baking dish and fill with the broccoli florets. Pour the melted coconut oil over the broccoli and add in the sliced s. Toss together. Put the dish in the air fryer.
2. Cook at 380°F for seven minutes, stirring at the halfway point.
3. Place the broccoli in a bowl and drizzle the lemon juice over it.

Buttered Broccoli

Servings:4
Cooking Time:7 Minutes
Ingredients:
- 4 cups fresh broccoli florets
- 2 tablespoons butter, melted
- ¼ cup water
- Salt and black pepper, to taste

Directions:
1. Preheat the Air fryer to 400°F and grease an Air fryer basket.
2. Mix broccoli, butter, salt, and black pepper in a bowl and toss to coat well.
3. Place water at the bottom of Air fryer pan and arrange the broccoli florets into the Air fryer basket.
4. Cook for about 7 minutes and dish out in a bowl to serve hot.

Pizza Dough

Servings:4
Cooking Time: 1 Hour 10 Minutes, Plus 10 Minutes For Additional Batches
Ingredients:
- 2 cups all-purpose flour
- 1 tablespoon granulated sugar
- 1 tablespoon quick-rise yeast
- 4 tablespoons olive oil, divided
- ¾ cup warm water

Directions:
1. In a large bowl, mix flour, sugar, and yeast until combined. Add 2 tablespoons oil and warm water and mix until dough becomes smooth.
2. On a lightly floured surface, knead dough 10 minutes, then form into a smooth ball. Drizzle with remaining 2 tablespoons oil, then cover with plastic. Let dough rise 1 hour until doubled in size.
3. Preheat the air fryer to 320°F.
4. Separate dough into four pieces and press each into a 6" pan or air fryer pizza tray that has been spritzed with cooking oil.
5. Add any desired toppings. Place in the air fryer basket, working in batches as necessary, and cook 10 minutes until crust is brown at the edges and toppings are heated through. Serve warm.

Two-cheese Grilled Sandwiches

Servings: 2
Cooking Time: 30 Minutes
Ingredients:
- 4 sourdough bread slices
- 2 cheddar cheese slices
- 2 Swiss cheese slices
- 1 tbsp butter
- 2 dill pickles, sliced

Directions:
1. Preheat air fryer to 360°F. Smear both sides of the sourdough bread with butter and place them in the frying basket. Toast the bread for 6 minutes, flipping once.
2. Divide the cheddar cheese between 2 of the bread slices. Cover the remaining 2 bread slices with Swiss cheese slices. Bake for 10 more minutes until the cheeses have melted and lightly bubbled and the bread has golden brown. Set the cheddar-covered bread slices on a serving plate, cover with pickles, and top each with the Swiss-covered slices. Serve and enjoy!

Savory Herb Cloud Eggs

Servings:2
Cooking Time: 8 Minutes
Ingredients:
- 2 large eggs, whites and yolks separated
- ¼ teaspoon salt
- ¼ teaspoon dried oregano
- 2 tablespoons chopped fresh chives
- 2 teaspoons salted butter, melted

Directions:
1. In a large bowl, whip egg whites until stiff peaks form, about 3 minutes. Place egg whites evenly into two ungreased 4" ramekins. Sprinkle evenly with salt, oregano, and chives. Place 1 whole egg yolk in center of each ramekin and drizzle with butter.
2. Place ramekins into air fryer basket. Adjust the temperature to 350°F and set the timer for 8 minutes. Egg whites will be fluffy and browned when done. Serve warm.

Pesto Vegetable Skewers

Servings:8
Cooking Time: 8 Minutes
Ingredients:
- 1 medium zucchini, trimmed and cut into ½" slices
- ½ medium yellow onion, peeled and cut into 1" squares
- 1 medium red bell pepper, seeded and cut into 1" squares
- 16 whole cremini mushrooms
- ⅓ cup basil pesto
- ½ teaspoon salt
- ¼ teaspoon ground black pepper

Directions:
1. Divide zucchini slices, onion, and bell pepper into eight even portions. Place on 6" skewers for a total of eight kebabs. Add 2 mushrooms to each skewer and brush kebabs generously with pesto.
2. Sprinkle each kebab with salt and black pepper on all sides, then place into ungreased air fryer basket. Adjust the temperature to 375°F and set the timer for 8 minutes, turning kebabs halfway through cooking. Vegetables will be browned at the edges and tender-crisp when done. Serve warm.

Cheese And Bean Enchiladas

Servings:4
Cooking Time: 9 Minutes
Ingredients:
- 1 can pinto beans, drained and rinsed
- 1 ½ tablespoons taco seasoning
- 1 cup red enchilada sauce, divided
- 1 ½ cups shredded Mexican-blend cheese, divided
- 4 fajita-size flour tortillas

Directions:
1. Preheat the air fryer to 320°F.
2. In a large microwave-safe bowl, microwave beans for 1 minute. Mash half the beans and fold into whole beans. Mix in taco seasoning, ¼ cup enchilada sauce, and 1 cup cheese until well combined.
3. Place ¼ cup bean mixture onto each tortilla. Fold up one end about 1", then roll to close.
4. Place enchiladas into a 3-quart baking pan, pushing together as needed to make them fit. Pour remaining ¾ cup enchilada sauce over enchiladas and top with remaining ½ cup cheese.
5. Place pan in the air fryer basket and cook 8 minutes until cheese is brown and bubbling and the edges of tortillas are brown. Serve warm.

Home-style Cinnamon Rolls

Servings: 4
Cooking Time: 40 Minutes
Ingredients:
- ½ pizza dough
- 1/3 cup dark brown sugar
- ¼ cup butter, softened
- ½ tsp ground cinnamon

Directions:
1. Preheat air fryer to 360°F. Roll out the dough into a rectangle. Using a knife, spread the brown sugar and butter, covering all the edges, and sprinkle with cinnamon. Fold the long side of the dough into a log, then cut it into 8 equal pieces, avoiding compression. Place the rolls, spiral-side up, onto a parchment-lined sheet. Let rise for 20 minutes. Grease the rolls with cooking spray and Bake for 8 minutes until golden brown. Serve right away.

Cauliflower Steak With Thick Sauce

Servings:2
Cooking Time: 15 Minutes
Ingredients:
- ¼ cup almond milk
- ¼ teaspoon vegetable stock powder
- 1 cauliflower, sliced into two
- 1 tablespoon olive oil
- 2 tablespoons onion, chopped
- salt and pepper to taste

Directions:
1. Soak the cauliflower in salted water or brine for at least 2 hours.
2. Preheat the air fryer to 400°F.
3. Rinse the cauliflower and place inside the air fryer and cook for 15 minutes.
4. Meanwhile, heat oil in a skillet over medium flame. Sauté the onions and stir until translucent. Add the vegetable stock powder and milk.
5. Bring to boil and adjust the heat to low.
6. Allow the sauce to reduce and season with salt and pepper.
7. Place cauliflower steak on a plate and pour over sauce.

Effortless Mac `n´ Cheese

Servings: 4
Cooking Time: 15 Minutes
Ingredients:
- 1 cup heavy cream
- 1 cup milk
- ½ cup mozzarella cheese
- 2 tsp grated Parmesan cheese
- 16 oz cooked elbow macaroni

Directions:
1. Preheat air fryer to 400°F. Whisk the heavy cream, milk, mozzarella cheese, and Parmesan cheese until smooth in a bowl. Stir in the macaroni and pour into a baking dish. Cover with foil and Bake in the air fryer for 6 minutes. Remove foil and Bake until cooked through and bubbly, 3-5 minutes. Serve warm.

Avocado Rolls

Servings:5
Cooking Time: 15 Minutes
Ingredients:
- 10 egg roll wrappers
- 1 tomato, diced

- ¼ tsp pepper
- ½ tsp salt

Directions:
1. Place all filling ingredients in a bowl; mash with a fork until somewhat smooth. There should be chunks left. Divide the feeling between the egg wrappers. Wet your finger and brush along the edges, so the wrappers can seal well. Roll and seal the wrappers.
2. Arrange them on a baking sheet lined dish, and place in the air fryer. Cook at 350°F for 5 minutes. Serve with sweet chili dipping and enjoy.

Honey Pear Chips

Servings: 4
Cooking Time: 30 Minutes
Ingredients:
- 2 firm pears, thinly sliced
- 1 tbsp lemon juice
- ½ tsp ground cinnamon
- 1 tsp honey

Directions:
1. Preheat air fryer to 380°F. Arrange the pear slices on the parchment-lined cooking basket. Drizzle with lemon juice and honey and sprinkle with cinnamon. Air Fry for 6-8 minutes, shaking the basket once, until golden. Leave to cool. Serve immediately or save for later in an airtight container. Good for 2 days.

Spinach Pesto Flatbread

Servings:4
Cooking Time: 8 Minutes Per Batch
Ingredients:
- 1 cup basil pesto
- 4 round flatbreads
- ½ cup chopped frozen spinach, thawed and drained
- 8 ounces fresh mozzarella cheese, sliced
- 1 teaspoon crushed red pepper flakes

Directions:
1. Preheat the air fryer to 350°F.
2. For each flatbread, spread ¼ cup pesto across flatbread, then scatter 2 tablespoons spinach over pesto. Top with 2 ounces mozzarella slices and ¼ teaspoon red pepper flakes. Repeat with remaining flatbread and toppings.
3. Place in the air fryer basket, working in batches as necessary, and cook 8 minutes until cheese is brown and bubbling. Serve warm.

Grilled 'n Glazed Strawberries

Servings:2

Cooking Time: 20 Minutes

Ingredients:

- 1 tbsp honey
- 1 tsp lemon zest
- 1-lb large strawberries
- 3 tbsp melted butter
- Lemon wedges
- Pinch kosher salt

Directions:

1. Thread strawberries in 4 skewers.

2. In a small bowl, mix well remaining ingredients except for lemon wedges. Brush all over strawberries.

3. Place skewer on air fryer skewer rack.

4. For 10 minutes, cook on 360°F. Halfway through cooking time, brush with honey mixture and turnover skewer.

5. Serve and enjoy with a squeeze of lemon.

White Cheddar And Mushroom Soufflés

Servings:4

Cooking Time: 12 Minutes

Ingredients:

- 3 large eggs, whites and yolks separated
- ½ cup sharp white Cheddar cheese
- 3 ounces cream cheese, softened
- ¼ teaspoon cream of tartar
- ¼ teaspoon salt
- ¼ teaspoon ground black pepper
- ½ cup cremini mushrooms, sliced

Directions:

1. In a large bowl, whip egg whites until stiff peaks form, about 2 minutes. In a separate large bowl, beat Cheddar, egg yolks, cream cheese, cream of tartar, salt, and pepper together until combined.

2. Fold egg whites into cheese mixture, being careful not to stir. Fold in mushrooms, then pour mixture evenly into four ungreased 4" ramekins.

3. Place ramekins into air fryer basket. Adjust the temperature to 350°F and set the timer for 12 minutes. Eggs will be browned on the top and firm in the center when done. Serve warm.

Sautéed Spinach

Servings:2

Cooking Time:9 Minutes

Ingredients:

- 1 small onion, chopped
- 6 ounces fresh spinach
- 2 tablespoons olive oil
- 1 teaspoon ginger, minced
- Salt and black pepper, to taste

Directions:

1. Preheat the Air fryer to 360°F and grease an Air fryer pan.

2. Put olive oil, onions and ginger in the Air fryer pan and place in the Air fryer basket.

3. Cook for about 4 minutes and add spinach, salt, and black pepper.

4. Cook for about 4 more minutes and dish out in a bowl to serve.

Vegetable Side Dishes Recipes

Herbed Croutons With Brie Cheese

Servings:1
Cooking Time: 20 Minutes
Ingredients:

- 1 tbsp french herbs
- 7 oz brie cheese, chopped
- 2 slices bread, halved

Directions:

1. Preheat air fryer to 340°F. In a bowl, mix oil with herbs. Brush the bread slices with oil mixture. Place on a flat surface. Top with brie cheese. Place in air fryer's basket; cook for 7 minutes. Cut into cubes.

Spiced Pumpkin Wedges

Servings: 4
Cooking Time: 35 Minutes
Ingredients:

- 2 ½ cups pumpkin, cubed
- 2 tbsp olive oil
- Salt and pepper to taste
- ¼ tsp pumpkin pie spice
- 1 tbsp thyme
- ¼ cup grated Parmesan

Directions:

1. Preheat air fryer to 360°F. Put the cubed pumpkin with olive oil, salt, pumpkin pie spice, black pepper, and thyme in a bowl and stir until the pumpkin is well coated. Pour this mixture into the frying basket and Roast for 18-20 minutes, stirring once. Sprinkle the pumpkin with grated Parmesan. Serve and enjoy!

Honey-mustard Asparagus Puffs

Servings: 4
Cooking Time: 35 Minutes
Ingredients:

- 8 asparagus spears
- ½ sheet puff pastry
- 2 tbsp honey mustard
- 1 egg, lightly beaten

Directions:

1. Preheat the air fryer to 375°F. Spread the pastry with honey mustard and cut it into 8 strips. Wrap the pastry, honey mustard–side in, around the asparagus.

Put a rack in the frying basket and lay the asparagus spears on the rack. Brush all over pastries with beaten egg and Air Fry for 12-17 minutes or until the pastry is golden. Serve.

Brussels Sprouts

Servings: 3
Cooking Time: 5 Minutes
Ingredients:

- 1 10-ounce package frozen brussels sprouts, thawed and halved
- 2 teaspoons olive oil
- salt and pepper

Directions:

1. Toss the brussels sprouts and olive oil together.
2. Place them in the air fryer basket and season to taste with salt and pepper.
3. Cook at 360°F for approximately 5minutes, until the edges begin to brown.

Zucchini Fries

Servings: 3
Cooking Time: 12 Minutes
Ingredients:

- 1 large Zucchini
- ½ cup All-purpose flour or tapioca flour
- 2 Large egg(s), well beaten
- 1 cup Seasoned Italian-style dried bread crumbs (gluten-free, if a concern)
- Olive oil spray

Directions:

1. Preheat the air fryer to 400°F.
2. Trim the zucchini into a long rectangular block, taking off the ends and four "sides" to make this shape. Cut the block lengthwise into ½-inch-thick slices. Lay these slices flat and cut in half widthwise. Slice each of these pieces into ½-inch-thick batons.
3. Set up and fill three shallow soup plates or small pie plates on your counter: one for the flour, one for the beaten egg(s), and one for the bread crumbs.
4. Set a zucchini baton in the flour and turn it several times to coat all sides. Gently shake off any excess flour, then dip it in the egg(s), turning it to coat. Let any excess egg slip back into the rest, then set the baton in the bread crumbs and turn it several times, pressing gently to coat all sides, even the ends. Set aside on a

cutting board and continue coating the remainder of the batons in the same way.

5.   Lightly coat the batons on all sides with olive oil spray. Set them in two flat layers in the basket, the top layer at a 90-degree angle to the bottom one, with a little air space between the batons in each layer. In the end, the whole thing will look like a crosshatch pattern. Air-fry undisturbed for 6 minutes.

6.   Use kitchen tongs to gently rearrange the batons so that any covered parts are now uncovered. The batons no longer need to be in a crosshatch pattern. Continue air-frying undisturbed for 6 minutes, or until lightly browned and crisp.

7.   Gently pour the contents of the basket onto a wire rack. Spread the batons out and cool for only a minute or two before serving.

Buttered Brussels Sprouts

Servings: 4
Cooking Time: 30 Minutes
Ingredients:
- ¼ cup grated Parmesan
- 2 tbsp butter, melted
- 1 lb Brussels sprouts
- Salt and pepper to taste

Directions:
1.   Preheat air fryer to 330°F. Trim the bottoms of the sprouts and remove any discolored leaves. Place the sprouts in a medium bowl along with butter, salt and pepper. Toss to coat, then place them in the frying basket. Roast for 20 minutes, shaking the basket twice. When done, the sprouts should be crisp with golden-brown color. Plate the sprouts in a serving dish and toss with Parmesan cheese.

Dijon Roast Cabbage

Servings:4
Cooking Time: 10 Minutes
Ingredients:
- 1 small head cabbage, cored and sliced into 1"-thick slices
- 2 tablespoons olive oil, divided
- ½ teaspoon salt
- 1 tablespoon Dijon mustard
- 1 teaspoon apple cider vinegar
- 1 teaspoon granular erythritol

Directions:
1.   Drizzle each cabbage slice with 1 tablespoon olive oil, then sprinkle with salt. Place slices into ungreased air fryer basket, working in batches if needed. Adjust the temperature to 350°F and set the timer for 10 minutes. Cabbage will be tender and edges will begin to brown when done.

2.   In a small bowl, whisk remaining olive oil with mustard, vinegar, and erythritol. Drizzle over cabbage in a large serving dish. Serve warm.

Cheesy Garlic Bread

Servings: 6
Cooking Time: 12 Minutes
Ingredients:
- 1 cup self-rising flour
- 1 cup plain full-fat Greek yogurt
- ¼ cup salted butter, softened
- 1 tablespoon minced garlic
- 1 cup shredded mozzarella cheese

Directions:
1.   Preheat the air fryer to 320°F. Cut parchment paper to fit the air fryer basket.

2.   In a large bowl, mix flour and yogurt until a sticky, soft dough forms. Let sit 5 minutes.

3.   Turn dough onto a lightly floured surface. Knead dough 1 minute, then transfer to prepared parchment. Press out into an 8" round.

4.   In a small bowl, mix butter and garlic. Brush over dough. Sprinkle with mozzarella.

5.   Place in the air fryer and cook 12 minutes until edges are golden and cheese is brown. Serve warm.

Yeast Rolls

Servings:16
Cooking Time: 1 Hour 10 Minutes
Ingredients:
- 4 tablespoons salted butter
- ¼ cup granulated sugar
- 1 cup hot water
- 1 tablespoon quick-rise yeast
- 1 large egg
- 1 teaspoon salt
- 2 ½ cups all-purpose flour, divided
- Cooking spray

Directions:
1.   In a microwave-safe bowl, microwave butter 30 seconds until melted. Pour 2 tablespoons of butter into a large bowl. Add sugar, hot water, and yeast. Mix until yeast is dissolved.

2.   Using a rubber spatula, mix in egg, salt, and 2 ¼ cups flour. Dough will be very sticky.

3.   Cover bowl with plastic wrap and let rise in a warm place 1 hour.

4. Sprinkle remaining ¼ cup flour on dough and turn onto a lightly floured surface. Knead 2 minutes, then cut into sixteen even pieces.

5. Preheat the air fryer to 350°F. Spray a 6" round cake pan with cooking spray.

6. Sprinkle each roll with flour and arrange in pan. Brush with remaining melted butter. Place pan in the air fryer basket and cook 10 minutes until fluffy and golden on top. Serve warm.

Corn Muffins

Servings: 12
Cooking Time: 10 Minutes
Ingredients:

- ½ cup all-purpose flour
- ½ cup cornmeal
- ¼ cup granulated sugar
- ½ teaspoon baking powder
- ¼ cup salted butter, melted
- ½ cup buttermilk
- 1 large egg

Directions:

1. Preheat the air fryer to 350°F.

2. In a large bowl, whisk together flour, cornmeal, sugar, and baking powder.

3. Add butter, buttermilk, and egg to dry mixture. Stir until well combined.

4. Divide batter evenly among twelve silicone or aluminum muffin cups, filling cups about halfway. Working in batches as needed, place in the air fryer and cook 10 minutes until golden brown. Let cool 5 minutes before serving.

Spicy Fried Green Beans

Servings: 2
Cooking Time: 8 Minutes
Ingredients:

- 12 ounces green beans, trimmed
- 2 small dried hot red chili peppers (like árbol)
- ¼ cup panko breadcrumbs
- 1 tablespoon olive oil
- ½ teaspoon salt
- ⅛ teaspoon crushed red pepper flakes
- 2 scallions, thinly sliced

Directions:

1. Preheat the air fryer to 400°F.

2. Toss the green beans, chili peppers and panko breadcrumbs with the olive oil, salt and crushed red pepper flakes.

3. Air-fry for 8 minutes, shaking the basket once during the cooking process. The crumbs will fall into the bottom drawer – don't worry.

4. Transfer the green beans to a serving dish, sprinkle the scallions and the toasted crumbs from the air fryer drawer on top and serve. The dried peppers are not to be eaten, but they do look nice with the green beans. You can leave them in, or take them out as you please.

"faux-tato" Hash

Servings:4
Cooking Time: 12 Minutes
Ingredients:

- 1 pound radishes, ends removed, quartered
- ¼ medium yellow onion, peeled and diced
- ½ medium green bell pepper, seeded and chopped
- 2 tablespoons salted butter, melted
- ½ teaspoon garlic powder
- ¼ teaspoon ground black pepper

Directions:

1. In a large bowl, combine radishes, onion, and bell pepper. Toss with butter.

2. Sprinkle garlic powder and black pepper over mixture in bowl, then spoon into ungreased air fryer basket.

3. Adjust the temperature to 320°F and set the timer for 12 minutes. Shake basket halfway through cooking. Radishes will be tender when done. Serve warm.

Turmeric Cabbage Mix

Servings: 4
Cooking Time: 12 Minutes
Ingredients:

- 1 tablespoon olive oil
- 1 big green cabbage head, shredded
- ½ cup yellow onion, chopped
- 2 teaspoons turmeric powder
- Salt and black pepper to taste
- 4 tablespoons tomato sauce

Directions:

1. Take the oil and grease a pan that fits your air fryer.

2. Add all of the other ingredients and toss.

3. Place the pan in the fryer and cook at 365°F for 12 minutes.

4. Divide between plates and serve as a side dish.

Rosemary Roasted Potatoes With Lemon

Servings: 4
Cooking Time: 12 Minutes
Ingredients:
- 1 pound small red-skinned potatoes, halved or cut into bite-sized chunks
- 1 tablespoon olive oil
- 1 teaspoon finely chopped fresh rosemary
- ¼ teaspoon salt
- freshly ground black pepper
- 1 tablespoon lemon zest

Directions:
1. Preheat the air fryer to 400°F.
2. Toss the potatoes with the olive oil, rosemary, salt and freshly ground black pepper.
3. Air-fry for 12 minutes, tossing the potatoes a few times throughout the cooking process.
4. As soon as the potatoes are tender to a knifepoint, toss them with the lemon zest and more salt if desired.

Mini Hasselback Potatoes

Servings: 4
Cooking Time: 25 Minutes
Ingredients:
- 1½ pounds baby Yukon Gold potatoes
- 5 tablespoons butter, cut into very thin slices
- salt and freshly ground black pepper
- 1 tablespoon vegetable oil
- ¼ cup grated Parmesan cheese (optional)
- chopped fresh parsley or chives

Directions:
1. Preheat the air fryer to 400°F.
2. Make six to eight deep vertical slits across the top of each potato about three quarters of the way down. Make sure the slits are deep enough to allow the slices to spread apart a little, but don't cut all the way through the potato. Place a thin slice of butter between each of the slices and season generously with salt and pepper.
3. Transfer the potatoes to the air fryer basket. Pack them in next to each other. It's alright if some of the potatoes sit on top or rest on another potato. Air-fry for 20 minutes.
4. Spray or brush the potatoes with a little vegetable oil and sprinkle the Parmesan cheese on top. Air-fry for an additional 5 minutes. Garnish with chopped parsley or chives and serve hot.

Savory Roasted Carrots

Servings:4
Cooking Time: 12 Minutes
Ingredients:
- 1 pound baby carrots
- 2 tablespoons dry ranch seasoning
- 3 tablespoons salted butter, melted

Directions:
1. Preheat the air fryer to 360°F.
2. Place carrots into a 6" round baking dish. Sprinkle carrots with ranch seasoning and drizzle with butter. Gently toss to coat.
3. Place in the air fryer basket and cook 12 minutes, stirring twice during cooking, until carrots are tender. Serve warm.

Simple Peppared Carrot Chips

Servings: 4
Cooking Time: 15 Minutes
Ingredients:
- 3 carrots, cut into coins
- 1 tbsp sesame oil
- Salt and pepper to taste

Directions:
1. Preheat air fryer at 375°F. Combine all ingredients in a bowl. Place carrots in the frying basket and Roast for 10 minutes, tossing once. Serve right away.

Crispy Brussels Sprouts

Servings: 3
Cooking Time: 12 Minutes
Ingredients:
- 1¼ pounds Medium, 2-inch-in-length Brussels sprouts
- 1½ tablespoons Olive oil
- ¾ teaspoon Table salt

Directions:
1. Preheat the air fryer to 400°F.
2. Halve each Brussels sprout through the stem end, pulling off and discarding any discolored outer leaves. Put the sprout halves in a large bowl, add the oil and salt, and stir well to coat evenly, until the Brussels sprouts are glistening.
3. When the machine is at temperature, scrape the contents of the bowl into the basket, gently spreading the Brussels sprout halves into as close to one layer as possible. Air-fry for 12 minutes, gently tossing and rearranging the vegetables twice to get all covered or touching parts exposed to the air currents, until crisp and browned at the edges.
4. Gently pour the contents of the basket onto a wire rack. Cool for a minute or two before serving.

Crunchy Green Beans

Servings: 4
Cooking Time: 15 Minutes
Ingredients:
- 1 tbsp tahini
- 1 tbsp lemon juice
- 1 tsp allspice
- 1 lb green beans, trimmed

Directions:
1. Preheat air fryer to 400°F. Whisk tahini, lemon juice, 1 tbsp of water, and allspice in a bowl. Put in the green beans and toss to coat. Roast for 5 minutes until golden brown and cooked. Serve immediately.

Garlic-parmesan French Fries

Servings:4
Cooking Time: 45 Minutes
Ingredients:
- 3 large russet potatoes, peeled, trimmed, and sliced into ½" × 4" sticks
- 2 ½ tablespoons olive oil, divided
- 2 teaspoons minced garlic
- ½ teaspoon salt
- ¼ teaspoon ground black pepper
- 1 teaspoon dried parsley
- ¼ cup grated Parmesan cheese

Directions:
1. Place potato sticks in a large bowl of cold water and let soak 30 minutes.
2. Preheat the air fryer to 350°F.
3. Drain potatoes and gently pat dry. Place in a large, dry bowl.
4. Pour 2 tablespoons oil over potatoes. Add garlic, salt, and pepper, then toss to fully coat.
5. Place fries in the air fryer basket and cook 15 minutes, shaking the basket twice during cooking, until fries are golden and crispy on the edges.
6. Place fries into a clean medium bowl and drizzle with remaining ½ tablespoon oil. Sprinkle parsley and Parmesan over fries and toss to coat. Serve warm.

Roasted Asparagus

Servings:4
Cooking Time: 12 Minutes
Ingredients:
- 1 tablespoon olive oil
- 1 pound asparagus spears, ends trimmed
- ¼ teaspoon salt
- ¼ teaspoon ground black pepper

- 1 tablespoon salted butter, melted

Directions:
1. In a large bowl, drizzle olive oil over asparagus spears and sprinkle with salt and pepper.
2. Place spears into ungreased air fryer basket. Adjust the temperature to 375°F and set the timer for 12 minutes, shaking the basket halfway through cooking. Asparagus will be lightly browned and tender when done.
3. Transfer to a large dish and drizzle with butter. Serve warm.

Easy Parmesan Asparagus

Servings: 4
Cooking Time: 15 Minutes
Ingredients:
- 3 tsp grated Parmesan cheese
- 1 lb asparagus, trimmed
- 2 tsp olive oil
- Salt to taste
- 1 clove garlic, minced
- ½ lemon

Directions:
1. Preheat air fryer at 375°F. Toss the asparagus and olive oil in a bowl, place them in the frying basket, and Air Fry for 8-10 minutes, tossing once. Transfer them into a large serving dish. Sprinkle with salt, garlic, and Parmesan cheese and toss until coated. Serve immediately with a squeeze of lemon. Enjoy!

Roasted Yellow Squash And Onions

Servings: 3
Cooking Time: 20 Minutes
Ingredients:
- 1 medium squash Yellow or summer crookneck squash, cut into ½-inch-thick rounds
- 1½ cups Yellow or white onion, roughly chopped
- ¾ teaspoon Table salt
- ¼ teaspoon Ground cumin (optional)
- Olive oil spray
- 1½ tablespoons Lemon or lime juice

Directions:
1. Preheat the air fryer to 375°F.
2. Toss the squash rounds, onion, salt, and cumin in a large bowl. Lightly coat the vegetables with olive oil spray, toss again, spray again, and keep at it until the vegetables are evenly coated.

3. When the machine is at temperature, scrape the contents of the bowl into the basket, spreading the vegetables out into as close to one layer as you can. Air-fry for 20 minutes, tossing once very gently, until the squash and onions are soft, even a little browned at the edges.

4. Pour the contents of the basket into a serving bowl, add the lemon or lime juice, and toss gently but well to coat. Serve warm or at room temperature.

Cheesy Vegetarian Lasagna

Servings: 4
Cooking Time: 40 Minutes
Ingredients:
- 1 ¼ cups shredded Italian-blend cheese, divided
- ½ cup grated vegetarian Parmesan cheese, divided
- ½ cup full-fat ricotta cheese
- ½ teaspoon salt
- ¼ teaspoon ground black pepper
- 2 cups tomato pasta sauce, divided
- 5 no-boil lasagna noodles

Directions:
1. Preheat the air fryer to 360°F. Spritz a 6" round baking pan with cooking spray.

2. In a medium bowl, mix 1 cup Italian-blend cheese, ¼ cup Parmesan, ricotta, salt, and pepper.

3. Pour ½ cup pasta sauce into the bottom of the prepared pan. Break the noodles into pieces to fit the pan. Place a layer of noodles into the pan.

4. Separate ricotta mixture into three portions. Spread one-third of the mixture over noodles in the pan. Pour ½ cup pasta sauce over ricotta mixture. Repeat layers of noodles, cheese mixture, and pasta sauce twice more until all ingredients are used, topping the final layer with remaining Italian-blend cheese.

5. Cover pan tightly with foil, being sure to tuck foil under the bottom of the pan to ensure the air fryer fan does not blow it off. Place in the air fryer basket. Cook 35 minutes, then remove foil and cook an additional 5 minutes until the top is golden brown and noodles are fork-tender.

6. Remove from the air fryer basket and top with remaining Parmesan and let cool 5 minutes before serving.

Asiago Broccoli

Servings: 4
Cooking Time: 14 Minutes
Ingredients:
- 1 head broccoli, cut into florets
- 1 tablespoon extra-virgin olive oil
- 1 teaspoon minced garlic
- ¼ teaspoon ground black pepper
- ¼ teaspoon salt
- ¼ cup asiago cheese

Directions:
1. Preheat the air fryer to 360°F.

2. In a medium bowl, toss the broccoli florets with the olive oil, garlic, pepper, and salt. Lightly spray the air fryer basket with olive oil spray.

3. Place the broccoli florets into the basket and cook for 7 minutes. Shake the basket and sprinkle the broccoli with cheese. Cook another 7 minutes.

4. Remove from the basket and serve warm.

Bacon-balsamic Brussels Sprouts

Servings:4
Cooking Time: 12 Minutes
Ingredients:
- 2 cups trimmed and halved fresh Brussels sprouts
- 2 tablespoons olive oil
- ¼ teaspoon salt
- ¼ teaspoon ground black pepper
- 2 tablespoons balsamic vinegar
- 2 slices cooked sugar-free bacon, crumbled

Directions:
1. In a large bowl, toss Brussels sprouts in olive oil, then sprinkle with salt and pepper. Place into ungreased air fryer basket. Adjust the temperature to 375°F and set the timer for 12 minutes, shaking the basket halfway through cooking. Brussels sprouts will be tender and browned when done.

2. Place sprouts in a large serving dish and drizzle with balsamic vinegar. Sprinkle bacon over top. Serve warm.

Flatbread Dippers

Servings:12

Cooking Time: 8 Minutes

Ingredients:

- 1 cup shredded mozzarella cheese
- 1 ounce cream cheese, broken into small pieces
- ½ cup blanched finely ground almond flour

Directions:

1. Place mozzarella into a large microwave-safe bowl. Add cream cheese pieces. Microwave on high 60 seconds, then stir to combine. Add flour and stir until a soft ball of dough forms.

2. Cut dough ball into two equal pieces. Cut a piece of parchment to fit into air fryer basket. Press each dough piece into a 5" round on ungreased parchment.

3. Place parchment with dough into air fryer basket. Adjust the temperature to 350°F and set the timer for 8 minutes. Carefully flip the flatbread over halfway through cooking. Flatbread will be golden brown when done.

4. Let flatbread cool 5 minutes, then slice each round into six triangles. Serve warm.

Tomato Candy

Servings: 12

Cooking Time: 120 Minutes

Ingredients:

- 6 Small Roma or plum tomatoes, halved lengthwise
- 1½ teaspoons Coarse sea salt or kosher salt

Directions:

1. Before you turn the machine on, set the tomatoes cut side up in a single layer in the basket. They can touch each other, but try to leave at least a fraction of an inch between them. Sprinkle the cut sides of the tomatoes with the salt.

2. Set the machine to cook at 225°F. Put the basket in the machine and air-fry for 2 hours, or until the tomatoes are dry but pliable, with a little moisture down in their centers.

3. Remove the basket from the machine and cool the tomatoes in it for 10 minutes before gently transferring them to a plate for serving, or to a shallow dish that you can cover and store in the refrigerator for up to 1 week.

Grilled Cheese

Servings: 2

Cooking Time: 25 Minutes

Ingredients:

- 4 slices bread
- ½ cup sharp cheddar cheese
- ¼ cup butter, melted

Directions:

1. Pre-heat the Air Fryer at 360°F.

2. Put cheese and butter in separate bowls.

3. Apply the butter to each side of the bread slices with a brush.

4. Spread the cheese across two of the slices of bread and make two sandwiches. Transfer both to the fryer.

5. Cook for 5 – 7 minutes or until a golden brown color is achieved and the cheese is melted.

Roasted Heirloom Carrots With Orange And Thyme

Servings: 2

Cooking Time: 12 Minutes

Ingredients:

- 10 to 12 heirloom or rainbow carrots, scrubbed but not peeled
- 1 teaspoon olive oil
- salt and freshly ground black pepper
- 1 tablespoon butter
- 1 teaspoon fresh orange zest
- 1 teaspoon chopped fresh thyme

Directions:

1. Preheat the air fryer to 400°F.

2. Scrub the carrots and halve them lengthwise. Toss them in the olive oil, season with salt and freshly ground black pepper and transfer to the air fryer.

3. Air-fry at 400°F for 12 minutes, shaking the basket every once in a while to rotate the carrots as they cook.

4. As soon as the carrots have finished cooking, add the butter, orange zest and thyme and toss all the ingredients together in the air fryer basket to melt the butter and coat evenly. Serve warm.

Burger Bun For One

Servings:1
Cooking Time: 5 Minutes
Ingredients:

- 2 tablespoons salted butter, melted
- ¼ cup blanched finely ground almond flour
- ¼ teaspoon baking powder
- ⅛ teaspoon apple cider vinegar
- 1 large egg, whisked

Directions:

1. Pour butter into an ungreased 4" ramekin. Add flour, baking powder, and vinegar to ramekin and stir until combined. Add egg and stir until batter is mostly smooth.
2. Place ramekin into air fryer basket. Adjust the temperature to 350°F and set the timer for 5 minutes. When done, the center will be firm and the top slightly browned. Let cool, about 5 minutes, then remove from ramekin and slice in half. Serve.

Cauliflower Rice Balls

Servings:4
Cooking Time: 8 Minutes
Ingredients:

- 1 steamer bag cauliflower rice, cooked according to package instructions
- ½ cup shredded mozzarella cheese
- 1 large egg
- 2 ounces plain pork rinds, finely crushed
- ¼ teaspoon salt
- ½ teaspoon Italian seasoning

Directions:

1. Place cauliflower into a large bowl and mix with mozzarella.
2. Whisk egg in a separate medium bowl. Place pork rinds into another large bowl with salt and Italian seasoning.
3. Separate cauliflower mixture into four equal sections and form each into a ball. Carefully dip a ball into whisked egg, then roll in pork rinds. Repeat with remaining balls.
4. Place cauliflower balls into ungreased air fryer basket. Adjust the temperature to 400°F and set the timer for 8 minutes. Rice balls will be golden when done.
5. Use a spatula to carefully move cauliflower balls to a large dish for serving. Serve warm.

Savory Brussels Sprouts

Servings: 4
Cooking Time: 15 Minutes
Ingredients:

- 1 lb Brussels sprouts, quartered
- 2 tbsp balsamic vinegar
- 1 tbsp olive oil
- 1 tbsp honey
- Salt and pepper to taste
- 1 ½ tbsp lime juice
- Parsley for sprinkling

Directions:

1. Preheat air fryer at 350°F. Combine all ingredients in a bowl. Transfer them to the frying basket. Air Fry for 10 minutes, tossing once. Top with lime juice and parsley.

Green Beans And Tomatoes Recipe

Servings: 4
Cooking Time:25 Minutes
Ingredients:

- 1-pint cherry tomatoes
- 2 tbsp. olive oil
- 1 lb. green beans
- Salt and black pepper to the taste

Directions:

1. In a bowl; mix cherry tomatoes with green beans, olive oil, salt and pepper, toss, transfer to your air fryer and cook at 400 °F, for 15 minutes. Divide among plates and serve right away

Pancetta Mushroom & Onion Sautée

Servings:4
Cooking Time: 20 Minutes
Ingredients:

- 16 oz white button mushrooms, stems trimmed, halved
- 1 onion, cut into half-moons
- 4 pancetta slices, diced
- 1 clove garlic, minced

Directions:

1. Preheat air fryer to 350°F. Add all ingredients, except for the garlic, to the frying basket and Air Fry for 8 minutes, tossing once. Stir in the garlic and cook for 1 more minute. Serve right away.

Fried Corn On The Cob

Servings: 2

Cooking Time: 10 Minutes

Ingredients:

- 1½ tablespoons Regular or low-fat mayonnaise (not fat-free; gluten-free, if a concern)
- 1½ teaspoons Minced garlic
- ¼ teaspoon Table salt
- ¾ cup Plain panko bread crumbs (gluten-free, if a concern)
- 3 4-inch lengths husked and de-silked corn on the cob
- Vegetable oil spray

Directions:

1. Preheat the air fryer to 400°F.
2. Stir the mayonnaise, garlic, and salt in a small bowl until well combined. Spread the panko on a dinner plate.
3. Brush the mayonnaise mixture over the kernels of a piece of corn on the cob. Set the corn in the bread crumbs, then roll, pressing gently, to coat it. Lightly coat with vegetable oil spray. Set it aside, then coat the remaining piece(s) of corn in the same way.
4. Set the coated corn on the cob in the basket with as much air space between the pieces as possible. Air-fry undisturbed for 10 minutes, or until brown and crisp along the coating.
5. Use kitchen tongs to gently transfer the pieces of corn to a wire rack. Cool for 5 minutes before serving.

Dinner Rolls

Servings:6

Cooking Time: 12 Minutes

Ingredients:

- 1 cup shredded mozzarella cheese
- 1 ounce cream cheese, broken into small pieces
- 1 cup blanched finely ground almond flour
- ¼ cup ground flaxseed
- ½ teaspoon baking powder
- 1 large egg, whisked

Directions:

1. Place mozzarella, cream cheese, and flour in a large microwave-safe bowl. Microwave on high 1 minute. Mix until smooth.
2. Add flaxseed, baking powder, and egg to mixture until fully combined and smooth. Microwave an additional 15 seconds if dough becomes too firm.
3. Separate dough into six equal pieces and roll each into a ball. Place rolls into ungreased air fryer basket.

Adjust the temperature to 320°F and set the timer for 12 minutes, turning rolls halfway through cooking. Allow rolls to cool completely before serving, about 5 minutes.

Baked Jalapeño And Cheese Cauliflower Mash

Servings:6

Cooking Time: 15 Minutes

Ingredients:

- 1 steamer bag cauliflower florets, cooked according to package instructions
- 2 tablespoons salted butter, softened
- 2 ounces cream cheese, softened
- ½ cup shredded sharp Cheddar cheese
- ¼ cup pickled jalapeños
- ½ teaspoon salt
- ¼ teaspoon ground black pepper

Directions:

1. Place cooked cauliflower into a food processor with remaining ingredients. Pulse twenty times until cauliflower is smooth and all ingredients are combined.
2. Spoon mash into an ungreased 6" round nonstick baking dish. Place dish into air fryer basket. Adjust the temperature to 380°F and set the timer for 15 minutes. The top will be golden brown when done. Serve warm.

Lemon Tempeh

Servings: 4

Cooking Time: 12 Minutes

Ingredients:

- 1 teaspoon lemon juice
- 1 tablespoon sunflower oil
- ¼ teaspoon ground coriander
- 6 oz tempeh, chopped

Directions:

1. Sprinkle the tempeh with lemon juice, sunflower oil, and ground coriander. Massage the tempeh gently with the help of the fingertips. After this, preheat the air fryer to 325°F. Put the tempeh in the air fryer and cook it for 12 minutes. Flip the tempeh every 2 minutes during cooking.

Bacon-wrapped Asparagus

Servings: 4
Cooking Time: 10 Minutes
Ingredients:
- 1 tablespoon extra-virgin olive oil
- ½ teaspoon sea salt
- ¼ cup grated Parmesan cheese
- 1 pound asparagus, ends trimmed
- 8 slices bacon

Directions:
1. Preheat the air fryer to 380°F.
2. In large bowl, mix together the olive oil, sea salt, and Parmesan cheese. Toss the asparagus in the olive oil mixture.
3. Evenly divide the asparagus into 8 bundles. Wrap 1 piece of bacon around each bundle, not overlapping the bacon but spreading it across the bundle.
4. Place the asparagus bundles into the air fryer basket, not touching. Work in batches as needed.
5. Cook for 8 minutes; check for doneness, and cook another 2 minutes.

Mini Spinach And Sweet Pepper Poppers

Servings:16
Cooking Time: 8 Minutes
Ingredients:
- 4 ounces cream cheese, softened
- 1 cup chopped fresh spinach leaves
- ½ teaspoon garlic powder
- 8 mini sweet bell peppers, tops removed, seeded, and halved lengthwise

Directions:
1. In a medium bowl, mix cream cheese, spinach, and garlic powder. Place 1 tablespoon mixture into each sweet pepper half and press down to smooth.
2. Place poppers into ungreased air fryer basket. Adjust the temperature to 400°F and set the timer for 8 minutes. Poppers will be done when cheese is browned on top and peppers are tender-crisp. Serve warm.

Asparagus

Servings: 4
Cooking Time: 9 Minutes
Ingredients:
- 1 bunch asparagus, washed and trimmed
- ⅛ teaspoon dried tarragon, crushed
- salt and pepper

- 1 to 2 teaspoons extra-light olive oil

Directions:
1. Spread asparagus spears on cookie sheet or cutting board.
2. Sprinkle with tarragon, salt, and pepper.
3. Drizzle with 1 teaspoon of oil and roll the spears or mix by hand. If needed, add up to 1 more teaspoon of oil and mix again until all spears are lightly coated.
4. Place spears in air fryer basket. If necessary, bend the longer spears to make them fit. It doesn't matter if they don't lie flat.
5. Cook at 390°F for 5minutes. Shake basket or stir spears with a spoon.
6. Cook for an additional 4 minutes or just until crisp-tender.

Lemon And Butter Artichokes

Servings: 4
Cooking Time: 15 Minutes
Ingredients:
- 12 ounces artichoke hearts
- Juice of ½ lemon
- 4 tablespoons butter, melted
- 2 tablespoons tarragon, chopped
- Salt and black pepper to the taste

Directions:
1. In a bowl, mix all the ingredients, toss, transfer the artichokes to your air fryer's basket and cook at 370°F for 15 minutes. Divide between plates and serve as a side dish.

Mouth-watering Provençal Mushrooms

Servings: 4
Cooking Time: 35 Minutes
Ingredients:
- 2 lb mushrooms, quartered
- 2-3 tbsp olive oil
- ½ tsp garlic powder
- 2 tsp herbs de Provence
- 2 tbsp dry white wine

Directions:
1. Preheat air fryer to 320°F. Beat together the olive oil, garlic powder, herbs de Provence, and white wine in a bowl. Add the mushrooms and toss gently to coat. Spoon the mixture onto the frying basket and Bake for 16-18 minutes, stirring twice. Serve hot and enjoy!

Spicy Roasted Potatoes

Servings: 2
Cooking Time: 15 Minutes
Ingredients:
- 4 potatoes, peeled and cut into wedges
- 2 tablespoons olive oil
- Sea salt and ground black pepper, to taste
- 1 teaspoon cayenne pepper
- 1/2 teaspoon ancho chili powder

Directions:
1. Toss all ingredients in a mixing bowl until the potatoes are well covered.
2. Transfer them to the Air Fryer basket and cook at 400°F for 6 minutes; shake the basket and cook for a further 6 minutes.
3. Serve warm with your favorite sauce for dipping. Bon appétit!

Simple Zucchini Ribbons

Servings:4
Cooking Time: 15 Minutes
Ingredients:
- 2 zucchini
- 2 tsp butter, melted
- ¼ tsp garlic powder
- ¼ tsp chili flakes
- 8 cherry tomatoes, halved
- Salt and pepper to taste

Directions:
1. Preheat air fryer to 275°F. Cut the zucchini into ribbons with a vegetable peeler. Mix them with butter, garlic, chili flakes, salt, and pepper in a bowl. Transfer to the frying basket and Air Fry for 2 minutes. Toss and add the cherry tomatoes. Cook for another 2 minutes. Serve.

Balsamic Green Beans With Bacon

Servings:4
Cooking Time: 15 Minutes
Ingredients:
- 2 cups green beans, trimmed
- 1 tbsp butter, melted
- Salt and pepper to taste
- 1 bacon slice, diced
- 1 clove garlic, minced
- 1 tbsp balsamic vinegar

Directions:
1. Preheat air fryer to 375°F. Combine green beans, butter, salt, and pepper in a bowl. Put the bean mixture in the frying basket and Air Fry for 5 minutes. Stir in bacon and Air Fry for 4 more minutes. Mix in garlic and cook for 1 minute. Transfer it to a serving dish, drizzle with balsamic vinegar and combine. Serve right away.

Roasted Broccoli

Servings:4
Cooking Time: 8 Minutes
Ingredients:
- 12 ounces broccoli florets
- 2 tablespoons olive oil
- ½ teaspoon salt
- ¼ teaspoon ground black pepper

Directions:
1. Preheat the air fryer to 360°F.
2. In a medium bowl, place broccoli and drizzle with oil. Sprinkle with salt and pepper.
3. Place in the air fryer basket and cook 8 minutes, shaking the basket twice during cooking, until the edges are brown and the center is tender. Serve warm.

Roasted Rhubarb

Servings: 4
Cooking Time: 15 Minutes
Ingredients:
- 1 pound rhubarb, cut in chunks
- 2 teaspoons olive oil
- 2 tablespoons orange zest
- ½ cup walnuts, chopped
- ½ teaspoon sugar

Directions:
1. In your air fryer, mix all the listed ingredients, and toss.
2. Cook at 380°F for 15 minutes.
3. Divide the rhubarb between plates and serve as a side dish.

Rosemary New Potatoes

Servings: 4
Cooking Time: 6 Minutes
Ingredients:
- 3 large red potatoes
- ¼ teaspoon ground rosemary
- ¼ teaspoon ground thyme
- ⅛ teaspoon salt
- ⅛ teaspoon ground black pepper
- 2 teaspoons extra-light olive oil

Directions:
1. Preheat air fryer to 330°F.
2. Place potatoes in large bowl and sprinkle with rosemary, thyme, salt, and pepper.
3. Stir with a spoon to distribute seasonings evenly.
4. Add oil to potatoes and stir again to coat well.
5. Cook at 330°F for 4minutes. Stir and break apart any that have stuck together.
6. Cook an additional 2 minutes or until fork-tender.

Beef , pork & Lamb Recipes

Empanadas

Servings:4
Cooking Time: 28 Minutes
Ingredients:
- 1 pound 80/20 ground beef
- ¼ cup taco seasoning
- ⅓ cup salsa
- 2 refrigerated piecrusts
- 1 cup shredded Colby-jack cheese

Directions:
1. In a medium skillet over medium heat, brown beef about 10 minutes until cooked through. Drain fat, then add taco seasoning and salsa to the pan. Bring to a boil, then cook 30 seconds. Reduce heat and simmer 5 minutes. Remove from heat.
2. Preheat the air fryer to 370°F.
3. Cut three 5" circles from each piecrust, forming six total. Reroll scraps out to ½" thickness. Cut out two more 5" circles to make eight circles total.
4. For each empanada, place ¼ cup meat mixture onto the lower half of a pastry circle and top with 2 tablespoons cheese. Dab a little water along the edge of pastry and fold circle in half to fully cover meat and cheese, pressing the edges together. Use a fork to gently seal the edges. Repeat with remaining pastry, meat, and cheese.
5. Spritz empanadas with cooking spray. Place in the air fryer basket and cook 12 minutes, turning halfway through cooking time, until crust is golden. Serve warm.

Crispy Pork Belly

Servings:4
Cooking Time: 20 Minutes
Ingredients:
- 1 pound pork belly, cut into 1" cubes
- ¼ cup soy sauce
- 1 tablespoon Worcestershire sauce
- 2 teaspoons sriracha hot chili sauce
- ½ teaspoon salt
- ¼ teaspoon ground black pepper

Directions:
1. Place pork belly into a medium sealable bowl or bag and pour in soy sauce, Worcestershire sauce, and sriracha. Seal and let marinate 30 minutes in the refrigerator.
2. Remove pork from marinade, pat dry with a paper towel, and sprinkle with salt and pepper.
3. Place pork in ungreased air fryer basket. Adjust the temperature to 360°F and set the timer for 20 minutes, shaking the basket halfway through cooking. Pork belly will be done when it has an internal temperature of at least 145°F and is golden brown.
4. Let pork belly rest on a large plate 10 minutes. Serve warm.

Grilled Prosciutto Wrapped Fig

Servings:2
Cooking Time: 8 Minutes
Ingredients:
- 2 whole figs, sliced in quarters
- 8 prosciutto slices
- Pepper and salt to taste

Directions:
1. Wrap a prosciutto slice around one slice of figs and then thread into skewer. Repeat process for remaining Ingredients. Place on skewer rack in air fryer.
2. For 8 minutes, cook on 390°F. Halfway through cooking time, turnover skewers.
3. Serve and enjoy.

Bacon Wrapped Filets Mignons

Servings: 4
Cooking Time: 18 Minutes
Ingredients:
- 4 slices bacon (not thick cut)
- 4 filets mignons
- 1 tablespoon fresh thyme leaves
- salt and freshly ground black pepper

Directions:
1. Preheat the air fryer to 400°F.
2. Lay the bacon slices down on a cutting board and sprinkle the thyme leaves on the bacon slices. Remove any string tying the filets and place the steaks down on their sides on top of the bacon slices. Roll the bacon around the side of the filets and secure the bacon to the fillets with a toothpick or two.
3. Season the steaks generously with salt and freshly ground black pepper and transfer the steaks to the air fryer.
4. Air-fry for 18 minutes, turning the steaks over halfway through the cooking process. This should cook your steaks to about medium, depending on how thick they are. If you'd prefer your steaks medium-rare or medium-well, simply add or subtract two minutes from the cooking time. Remove the steaks from the air fryer and let them rest for 5 minutes before removing the toothpicks and serving.

Pepperoni Pockets

Servings: 4
Cooking Time: 8 Minutes
Ingredients:
- 4 bread slices, 1-inch thick
- olive oil for misting
- 24 slices pepperoni
- 1 ounce roasted red peppers, drained and patted dry
- 1 ounce Pepper Jack cheese cut into 4 slices
- pizza sauce (optional)

Directions:
1. Spray both sides of bread slices with olive oil.
2. Stand slices upright and cut a deep slit in the top to create a pocket—almost to the bottom crust but not all the way through.
3. Stuff each bread pocket with 6 slices of pepperoni, a large strip of roasted red pepper, and a slice of cheese.
4. Place bread pockets in air fryer basket, standing up. Cook at 360°F for 8 minutes, until filling is heated through and bread is lightly browned. Serve while hot as is or with pizza sauce for dipping.

Lamb Burgers

Servings: 2
Cooking Time: 16 Minutes
Ingredients:
- 8 oz lamb, minced
- ½ teaspoon salt
- ½ teaspoon ground black pepper
- ½ teaspoon dried cilantro
- 1 tablespoon water
- Cooking spray

Directions:
1. In the mixing bowl mix up minced lamb, salt, ground black pepper, dried cilantro, and water.
2. Stir the meat mixture carefully with the help of the spoon and make 2 burgers.
3. Preheat the air fryer to 375°F.
4. Spray the air fryer basket with cooking spray and put the burgers inside.
5. Cook them for 8 minutes from each side.

Cheddar Bacon Ranch Pinwheels

Servings:5
Cooking Time: 12 Minutes Per Batch
Ingredients:
- 4 ounces full-fat cream cheese, softened
- 1 tablespoon dry ranch seasoning
- ½ cup shredded Cheddar cheese
- 1 sheet frozen puff pastry dough, thawed
- 6 slices bacon, cooked and crumbled

Directions:
1. Preheat the air fryer to 320°F. Cut parchment paper to fit the air fryer basket.
2. In a medium bowl, mix cream cheese, ranch seasoning, and Cheddar. Unfold puff pastry and gently spread cheese mixture over pastry.
3. Sprinkle crumbled bacon on top. Starting from a long side, roll dough into a log, pressing in the edges to seal.
4. Cut log into ten pieces, then place on parchment in the air fryer basket, working in batches as necessary.
5. Cook 12 minutes, turning each piece after 7 minutes. Let cool 5 minutes before serving.

Bacon And Blue Cheese Burgers

Servings:4
Cooking Time: 15 Minutes
Ingredients:
- 1 pound 70/30 ground beef
- 6 slices cooked sugar-free bacon, finely chopped
- ½ cup crumbled blue cheese
- ¼ cup peeled and chopped yellow onion
- ½ teaspoon salt
- ¼ teaspoon ground black pepper

Directions:
1. In a large bowl, mix ground beef, bacon, blue cheese, and onion. Separate into four sections and shape each section into a patty. Sprinkle with salt and pepper.
2. Place patties into ungreased air fryer basket. Adjust the temperature to 350°F and set the timer for 15 minutes, turning patties halfway through cooking. Burgers will be done when internal temperature is at least 150°F for medium and 180°F for well. Serve warm.

Bacon-wrapped Pork Tenderloin

Servings:6
Cooking Time: 20 Minutes
Ingredients:
- 1 pork tenderloin
- ½ teaspoon salt
- ½ teaspoon garlic powder
- ¼ teaspoon ground black pepper
- 8 slices sugar-free bacon

Directions:
1. Sprinkle tenderloin with salt, garlic powder, and pepper. Wrap each piece of bacon around tenderloin and secure with toothpicks.
2. Place tenderloin into ungreased air fryer basket. Adjust the temperature to 400°F and set the timer for 20 minutes, turning tenderloin after 15 minutes. When done, bacon will be crispy and tenderloin will have an internal temperature of at least 145°F.
3. Cut the tenderloin into six even portions and transfer each to a medium plate and serve warm.

Crispy Pierogi With Kielbasa And Onions

Servings: 3
Cooking Time: 20 Minutes
Ingredients:
- 6 Frozen potato and cheese pierogi, thawed
- ½ pound Smoked kielbasa, sliced into ½-inch-thick rounds
- ¾ cup Very roughly chopped sweet onion, preferably Vidalia
- Vegetable oil spray

Directions:
1. Preheat the air fryer to 375°F .
2. Put the pierogi, kielbasa rounds, and onion in a large bowl. Coat them with vegetable oil spray, toss well, spray again, and toss until everything is glistening.
3. When the machine is at temperature, dump the contents of the bowl it into the basket. Air-fry, tossing and rearranging everything twice so that all covered surfaces get exposed, for 20 minutes, or until the sausages have begun to brown and the pierogi are crisp.
4. Pour the contents of the basket onto a serving platter. Wait a minute or two just to take make sure nothing's searing hot before serving.

Bjorn's Beef Steak

Servings: 1
Cooking Time: 15 Minutes
Ingredients:

- 1 steak, 1-inch thick
- 1 tbsp. olive oil
- Black pepper to taste
- Sea salt to taste

Directions:

1. Place the baking tray inside the Air Fryer and pre-heat for about 5 minutes at 390°F.
2. Brush or spray both sides of the steak with the oil.
3. Season both sides with salt and pepper.
4. Take care when placing the steak in the baking tray and allow to cook for 3 minutes. Flip the meat over, and cook for an additional 3 minutes.
5. Take it out of the fryer and allow to sit for roughly 3 minutes before serving.

Fajita Flank Steak Rolls

Servings:4
Cooking Time: 12 Minutes
Ingredients:

- 1 pound flank steak
- 4 slices pepper jack cheese
- 1 medium green bell pepper, seeded and chopped
- ½ medium red bell pepper, seeded and chopped
- ¼ cup finely chopped yellow onion
- 1 teaspoon salt
- ½ teaspoon ground black pepper
- Cooking spray

Directions:

1. Preheat the air fryer to 400°F.
2. Carefully butterfly steak, leaving the two halves connected. Place slices of cheese on top of steak. Scatter bell peppers and onion over cheese in an even layer.
3. Place steak so that the grain runs horizontally. Tightly roll up steak and secure it with eight evenly spaced toothpicks or eight sections of butcher's twine.
4. Slice steak into four even rolls. Spritz with cooking spray, then sprinkle with salt and black pepper. Place in the air fryer basket and cook 12 minutes until steak is brown on the edges and internal temperature reaches at least 160°F for well-done. Serve.

Calzones

Servings:4
Cooking Time: 15 Minutes
Ingredients:

- 1 tube refrigerated pizza dough
- 28 slices pepperoni
- ½ cup full-fat ricotta cheese
- 1 cup shredded mozzarella cheese
- 1 large egg, whisked

Directions:

1. Preheat the air fryer to 350°F. Cut parchment paper to fit the air fryer basket.
2. Place dough on a work surface and unroll. Cut into four sections.
3. For each calzone, place 7 slices pepperoni on the bottom half of a dough section. Top pepperoni with 2 tablespoons ricotta and ¼ cup mozzarella.
4. Fold top half of dough over to cover the fillings and press the edges together. Gently roll the edges closed or press them with a fork to seal.
5. Brush calzones with egg. Place on parchment in the air fryer basket and cook 15 minutes, turning after about 10 minutes, until firm and golden brown. Serve warm.

Crunchy Veal Cutlets

Servings: 2
Cooking Time: 5 Minutes
Ingredients:

- ½ cup All-purpose flour or tapioca flour
- 1 Large egg(s), well beaten
- ¾ cup Seasoned Italian-style dried bread crumbs (gluten-free, if a concern)
- 2 tablespoons Yellow cornmeal
- 4 Thinly pounded 2-ounce veal leg cutlets (less than ¼ inch thick)
- Olive oil spray

Directions:

1. Preheat the air fryer to 400°F.
2. Set up and fill three shallow soup plates or small pie plates on your counter: one for the flour; one for the egg(s); and one for the bread crumbs, whisked with the cornmeal until well combined.
3. Dredge a veal cutlet in the flour, coating it on both sides. Gently shake off any excess flour, then gently dip it in the beaten egg(s), coating both sides. Let the excess egg slip back into the rest. Dip the cutlet in the bread-crumb mixture, turning it several times and pressing gently to make an even coating on both sides. Coat it on both sides with olive oil spray, then set it aside and continue dredging and coating more cutlets.
4. When the machine is at temperature, set the cutlets in the basket so that they don't touch each other. Air-fry undisturbed for 5 minutes, or until crisp and brown. (If only some of the veal cutlets will fit in one layer for any selected batch—the sizes of air fryer baskets vary dramatically—work in batches as necessary.)
5. Use kitchen tongs to transfer the cutlets to a wire rack. Cool for only 1 to 2 minutes before serving.

Almond And Sun-dried Tomato Crusted Pork Chops

Servings: 4
Cooking Time: 10 Minutes
Ingredients:

- ½ cup oil-packed sun-dried tomatoes
- ½ cup toasted almonds
- ¼ cup grated Parmesan cheese
- ½ cup olive oil
- 2 tablespoons water
- ½ teaspoon salt
- freshly ground black pepper
- 4 center-cut boneless pork chops

Directions:

1. Place the sun-dried tomatoes into a food processor and pulse them until they are coarsely chopped. Add the almonds, Parmesan cheese, olive oil, water, salt and pepper. Process all the ingredients into a smooth paste. Spread most of the paste onto both sides of the pork chops and then pierce the meat several times with a needle-style meat tenderizer or a fork. Let the pork chops sit and marinate for at least 1 hour.

2. Preheat the air fryer to 370°F.

3. Brush a little olive oil on the bottom of the air fryer basket. Transfer the pork chops into the air fryer basket, spooning a little more of the sun-dried tomato paste onto the pork chops if there are any gaps where the paste may have been rubbed off. Air-fry the pork chops at 370°F for 10 minutes, turning the chops over halfway through the cooking process.

4. When the pork chops have finished cooking, transfer them to a serving plate and serve with mashed potatoes and vegetables for a hearty meal.

Venison Backstrap

Servings: 4
Cooking Time: 10 Minutes
Ingredients:

- 2 eggs
- ¼ cup milk
- 1 cup whole wheat flour
- ½ teaspoon salt
- ¼ teaspoon pepper
- 1 pound venison backstrap, sliced
- salt and pepper
- oil for misting or cooking spray

Directions:

1. Beat together eggs and milk in a shallow dish.

2. In another shallow dish, combine the flour, salt, and pepper. Stir to mix well.

3. Sprinkle venison steaks with additional salt and pepper to taste. Dip in flour, egg wash, then in flour again, pressing in coating.

4. Spray steaks with oil or cooking spray on both sides.

5. Cooking in 2 batches, place steaks in the air fryer basket in a single layer. Cook at 360°F for 8minutes. Spray with oil, turn over, and spray other side. Cook for 2 minutes longer, until coating is crispy brown and meat is done to your liking.

6. Repeat to cook remaining venison.

7. Spray both sides with oil and cook for 5minutes. If needed, mist with oil and continue cooking for 3 minutes longer. This second batch will cook a little faster than the first because your air fryer is already hot.

8. Serve with marinara sauce on the side for dipping.

Sweet Potato–crusted Pork Rib Chops

Servings: 2
Cooking Time: 14 Minutes
Ingredients:

- 2 Large egg white(s), well beaten
- 1½ cups Crushed sweet potato chips (certified gluten-free, if a concern)
- 1 teaspoon Ground cinnamon
- 1 teaspoon Ground dried ginger
- 1 teaspoon Table salt (optional)
- 2 10-ounce, 1-inch-thick bone-in pork rib chop(s)

Directions:

1. Preheat the air fryer to 375°F .

2. Set up and fill two shallow soup plates or small pie plates on your counter: one for the beaten egg white(s); and one for the crushed chips, mixed with the cinnamon, ginger, and salt.

3. Dip a chop in the egg white(s), coating it on both sides as well as the edges. Let the excess egg white slip back into the rest, then set it in the crushed chip mixture. Turn it several times, pressing gently, until evenly coated on both sides and the edges. If necessary, set the chop aside and coat the remaining chop(s).

4. Set the chop(s) in the basket with as much air space between them as possible. Air-fry undisturbed for 12 minutes, or until crunchy and browned and an instant-read meat thermometer inserted into the center of a chop registers 145°F. If the machine is at 360°F, you may need to add 2 minutes to the cooking time.

5. Use kitchen tongs to transfer the chop(s) to a wire rack. Cool for 2 or 3 minutes before serving.

Crispy Smoked Pork Chops

Servings: 3
Cooking Time: 8 Minutes
Ingredients:

- ⅔ cup All-purpose flour or tapioca flour
- 1 Large egg white(s)
- 2 tablespoons Water
- 1½ cups Corn flake crumbs (gluten-free, if a concern)
- 3 ½-pound, ½-inch-thick bone-in smoked pork chops

Directions:

1. Preheat the air fryer to 375°F.
2. Set up and fill three shallow soup plates or small pie plates on your counter: one for the flour; one for the egg white(s), whisked with the water until foamy; and one for the corn flake crumbs.
3. Set a chop in the flour and turn it several times, coating both sides and the edges. Gently shake off any excess flour, then set it in the beaten egg white mixture. Turn to coat both sides as well as the edges. Let any excess egg white slip back into the rest, then set the chop in the corn flake crumbs. Turn it several times, pressing gently to coat the chop evenly on both sides and around the edge. Set the chop aside and continue coating the remaining chop(s) in the same way.
4. Set the chops in the basket with as much air space between them as possible. Air-fry undisturbed for 8 minutes, or until the coating is crunchy and the chops are heated through.
5. Use kitchen tongs to transfer the chops to a wire rack and cool for a couple of minutes before serving.

Steakhouse Filets Mignons

Servings: 3
Cooking Time: 12-15 Minutes
Ingredients:

- ¾ ounce Dried porcini mushrooms
- ¼ teaspoon Granulated white sugar
- ¼ teaspoon Ground white pepper
- ¼ teaspoon Table salt
- 6 ¼-pound filets mignons or beef tenderloin steaks
- 6 Thin-cut bacon strips (gluten-free, if a concern)

Directions:

1. Preheat the air fryer to 400°F.
2. Grind the dried mushrooms in a clean spice grinder until powdery. Add the sugar, white pepper, and salt. Grind to blend.
3. Rub this mushroom mixture into both cut sides of each filet. Wrap the circumference of each filet with a strip of bacon.
4. Set the filets mignons in the basket on their sides with the bacon seam side down. Do not let the filets touch; keep at least ¼ inch open between them. Air-fry undisturbed for 12 minutes for rare, or until an instant-read meat thermometer inserted into the center of a filet registers 125°F; 13 minutes for medium-rare, or until an instant-read meat thermometer inserted into the center of a filet registers 132°F; or 15 minutes for medium, or until an instant-read meat thermometer inserted into the center of a filet registers 145°F.
5. Use kitchen tongs to transfer the filets to a wire rack, setting them cut side down. Cool for 5 minutes before serving.

Friday Night Cheeseburgers

Servings: 4
Cooking Time: 20 Minutes
Ingredients:

- 1 lb ground beef
- 1 tsp Worcestershire sauce
- 1 tbsp allspice
- Salt and pepper to taste
- 4 cheddar cheese slices
- 4 buns

Directions:

1. Preheat air fryer to 360°F. Combine beef, Worcestershire sauce, allspice, salt and pepper in a large bowl. Divide into 4 equal portions and shape into patties. Place the burgers in the greased frying basket and Air Fry for 8 minutes. Flip and cook for another 3-4 minutes. Top each burger with cheddar cheese and cook for another minute so the cheese melts. Transfer to a bun and serve.

Stress-free Beef Patties

Servings: 2
Cooking Time: 30 Minutes
Ingredients:
- ½ lb ground beef
- 1 ½ tbsp ketchup
- 1 ½ tbsp tamari
- ½ tsp jalapeño powder
- ½ tsp mustard powder
- Salt and pepper to taste

Directions:
1. Preheat air fryer to 350°F.Add the beef, ketchup, tamari, jalapeño, mustard salt, and pepper in a bowl and mix until evenly combined. Shape into 2 patties, then place them on the greased frying basket. Air Fry for 18-20 minutes, turning once. Serve and enjoy!

Air Fried Thyme Garlic Lamb Chops

Servings: 4
Cooking Time: 12 Minutes
Ingredients:
- 4 lamb chops
- 4 garlic cloves, minced
- 3 tbsp olive oil
- 1 tbsp dried thyme
- Pepper
- Salt

Directions:
1. Preheat the air fryer to 390°F.   1 9 5
2. Season lamb chops with pepper and salt.
3. In a small bowl, mix together thyme, oil, and garlic and rub over lamb chops.
4. Place lamb chops into the air fryer and cook for 12 minutes. Turn halfway through.
5. Serve and enjoy.

Buttery Pork Chops

Servings:4
Cooking Time: 12 Minutes
Ingredients:
- 4 boneless pork chops
- 1 teaspoon salt
- ½ teaspoon ground black pepper
- 4 tablespoons salted butter, sliced into 8 (½-tablespoon) pats, divided

Directions:
1. Preheat the air fryer to 400°F.

2. Sprinkle pork chops with salt and pepper. Top each pork chop with a ½-tablespoon butter pat.
3. Place chops in the air fryer basket and cook 12 minutes, turning halfway through cooking time, until tops and edges are golden brown and internal temperature reaches at least 145°F.
4. Use remaining butter pats to top each pork chop while hot, then let cool 5 minutes before serving warm.

Brown Sugar Mustard Pork Loin

Servings:4
Cooking Time: 35 Minutes
Ingredients:
- 1 pound boneless pork loin
- 1 tablespoon olive oil
- ¼ cup Dijon mustard
- ¼ cup brown sugar
- 1 teaspoon salt
- ½ teaspoon ground black pepper

Directions:
1. Preheat the air fryer to 400°F. Brush pork loin with oil.
2. In a small bowl, mix mustard, brown sugar, salt, and pepper. Brush mixture over both sides of pork loin and let sit 15 minutes.
3. Place in the air fryer basket and cook 20 minutes until internal temperature reaches 145°F. Let rest 10 minutes before slicing. Serve warm.

Easy-peasy Beef Sliders

Servings:4
Cooking Time: 25 Minutes
Ingredients:
- 1 lb ground beef
- ¼ tsp cumin
- ¼ tsp mustard power
- 1/3 cup grated yellow onion
- ½ tsp smoked paprika
- Salt and pepper to taste

Directions:
1. Preheat air fryer to 350°F. Combine the ground beef, cumin, mustard, onion, paprika, salt, and black pepper in a bowl. Form mixture into 8 patties and make a slight indentation in the middle of each. Place beef patties in the greased frying basket and Air Fry for 8-10 minutes, flipping once. Serve right away and enjoy!

Marinated Steak Kebabs

Servings:4
Cooking Time: 5 Minutes
Ingredients:

- 1 pound strip steak, fat trimmed, cut into 1" cubes
- ½ cup soy sauce
- ¼ cup olive oil
- 1 tablespoon granular brown erythritol
- ½ teaspoon salt
- ¼ teaspoon ground black pepper
- 1 medium green bell pepper, seeded and chopped into 1" cubes

Directions:

1. Place steak into a large sealable bowl or bag and pour in soy sauce and olive oil. Add erythritol, then stir to coat steak. Marinate at room temperature 30 minutes.
2. Remove streak from marinade and sprinkle with salt and black pepper.
3. Place meat and vegetables onto 6" skewer sticks, alternating between steak and bell pepper.
4. Place kebabs into ungreased air fryer basket. Adjust the temperature to 400°F and set the timer for 5 minutes. Steak will be done when crispy at the edges and peppers are tender. Serve warm.

City "chicken"

Servings: 3
Cooking Time: 10 Minutes
Ingredients:

- 1 pound Pork tenderloin, cut into 2-inch cubes
- ½ cup All-purpose flour or tapioca flour
- 1 Large egg(s)
- 1 teaspoon Dried poultry seasoning blend
- 1¼ cups Plain panko bread crumbs (gluten-free, if a concern)
- Vegetable oil spray

Directions:

1. Preheat the air fryer to 350°F .
2. Thread 3 or 4 pieces of pork on a 4-inch bamboo skewer. You'll need 2 or 3 skewers for a small batch, 3 or 4 for a medium, and up to 6 for a large batch.
3. Set up and fill three shallow soup plates or small pie plates on your counter: one for the flour; one for the egg(s), beaten with the poultry seasoning until foamy; and one for the bread crumbs.
4. Dip and roll one skewer into the flour, coating all sides of the meat. Gently shake off any excess flour, then dip and roll the skewer in the egg mixture. Let any excess egg mixture slip back into the rest, then set the skewer in the bread crumbs and roll it around, pressing gently, until the exterior surfaces of the meat are evenly coated. Generously coat the meat on the skewer with vegetable oil spray. Set aside and continue dredging, dipping, coating, and spraying the remaining skewers.

5. Set the skewers in the basket in one layer and air-fry undisturbed for 10 minutes, or until brown and crunchy.
6. Use kitchen tongs to transfer the skewers to a wire rack. Cool for a minute or two before serving.

Honey-sriracha Pork Ribs

Servings:4
Cooking Time: 25 Minutes
Ingredients:

- 3 pounds pork back ribs, white membrane removed
- 2 teaspoons salt
- 1 teaspoon ground black pepper
- ½ cup sriracha
- ⅓ cup honey
- 1 tablespoon lemon juice

Directions:

1. Preheat the air fryer to 400°F.
2. Place ribs on a work surface and cut the rack into two pieces to fit in the air fryer basket.
3. Sprinkle ribs with salt and pepper and place in the air fryer basket meat side down. Cook 15 minutes.
4. In a small bowl, combine the sriracha, honey, and lemon juice to make a sauce.
5. Remove ribs from the air fryer basket and pour sauce over both sides. Return them to the air fryer basket meat side up and cook an additional 10 minutes until brown and the internal temperature reaches at least 190°F. Serve warm.

Blackened Steak Nuggets

Servings: 2

Cooking Time: 7 Minutes

Ingredients:

- 1 pound rib eye steak, cut into 1" cubes
- 2 tablespoons salted butter, melted
- ½ teaspoon paprika
- ½ teaspoon salt
- ¼ teaspoon garlic powder
- ¼ teaspoon onion powder
- ¼ teaspoon ground black pepper
- ⅛ teaspoon cayenne pepper

Directions:

1. Place steak into a large bowl and pour in butter. Toss to coat. Sprinkle with remaining ingredients.

2. Place bites into ungreased air fryer basket. Adjust the temperature to 400°F and set the timer for 7 minutes, shaking the basket three times during cooking. Steak will be crispy on the outside and browned when done and internal temperature is at least 150°F for medium and 180°F for well-done. Serve warm.

Mustard Beef Mix

Servings: 7

Cooking Time: 30 Minutes

Ingredients:

- 2-pound beef ribs, boneless
- 1 tablespoon Dijon mustard
- 1 tablespoon sunflower oil
- 1 teaspoon ground paprika
- 1 teaspoon cayenne pepper

Directions:

1. In the shallow bowl mix up Dijon mustard and sunflower oil. Then sprinkle the beef ribs with ground paprika and cayenne pepper. After this, brush the meat with Dijon mustard mixture and leave for 10 minutes to marinate. Meanwhile, preheat the air fryer to 400°F. Put the beef ribs in the air fryer to and cook them for 10 minutes. Then flip the ribs on another side and reduce the air fryer heat to 325°F. Cook the ribs for 20 minutes more.

Delicious Cheeseburgers

Servings: 4

Cooking Time: 12 Minutes

Ingredients:

- 1 lb ground beef
- 4 cheddar cheese slices
- 1/2 tsp Italian seasoning

- Pepper
- Salt
- Cooking spray

Directions:

1. Spray air fryer basket with cooking spray.

2. In a bowl, mix together ground beef, Italian seasoning, pepper, and salt.

3. Make four equal shapes of patties from meat mixture and place into the air fryer basket.

4. Cook at 375°F for 5 minutes. Turn patties to another side and cook for 5 minutes more.

5. Place cheese slices on top of each patty and cook for 2 minutes more.

6. Serve and enjoy.

Roasted Lamb

Servings: 4

Cooking Time: 1 Hour 30 Minutes

Ingredients:

- 2½ pounds half lamb leg roast, slits carved
- 2 garlic cloves, sliced into smaller slithers
- 1 tablespoon dried rosemary
- 1 tablespoon olive oil
- Cracked Himalayan rock salt and cracked peppercorns, to taste

Directions:

1. Preheat the Air fryer to 400°F and grease an Air fryer basket.

2. Insert the garlic slithers in the slits and brush with rosemary, oil, salt, and black pepper.

3. Arrange the lamb in the Air fryer basket and cook for about 15 minutes.

4. Set the Air fryer to 350°F on the Roast mode and cook for 1 hour and 15 minutes.

5. Dish out the lamb chops and serve hot.

Spice-coated Steaks

Servings: 2

Cooking Time: 15 Minutes

Ingredients:

- ½ tsp cayenne pepper
- 1 tbsp olive oil
- ½ tsp ground paprika
- Salt and black pepper to taste

Directions:

1. Preheat air fryer to 390°F. Mix olive oil, black pepper, cayenne, paprika, and salt and rub onto steaks. Spread evenly. Put the steaks in the fryer, and cook for 6 minutes, turning them halfway through.

Pork Chops

Servings: 2
Cooking Time: 16 Minutes
Ingredients:
- 2 bone-in, centercut pork chops, 1-inch thick
- 2 teaspoons Worcestershire sauce
- salt and pepper
- cooking spray

Directions:
1. Rub the Worcestershire sauce into both sides of pork chops.
2. Season with salt and pepper to taste.
3. Spray air fryer basket with cooking spray and place the chops in basket side by side.
4. Cook at 360°F for 16 minutes or until well done. Let rest for 5minutes before serving.

Salted 'n Peppered Scored Beef Chuck

Servings:6
Cooking Time: 1 Hour And 30 Minutes
Ingredients:
- 2 ounces black peppercorns
- 2 tablespoons olive oil
- 3 pounds beef chuck roll, scored with knife
- 3 tablespoons salt

Directions:
1. Preheat the air fryer to 390°F.
2. Place the grill pan accessory in the air fryer.
3. Season the beef chuck roll with black peppercorns and salt.
4. Brush with olive oil and cover top with foil.
5. Grill for 1 hour and 30 minutes.
6. Flip the beef every 30 minutes for even grilling on all sides.

Simple Pork Chops

Servings: 4
Cooking Time: 20 Minutes
Ingredients:
- 4 pork chops, boneless
- 1 1/2 tbsp Mr. Dash seasoning
- Pepper
- Salt

Directions:
1. Coat pork chops with Mr. dash seasoning, pepper, and salt.
2. Place pork chops in the air fryer and cook at 360°F for 10 minutes.

3. Turn pork chops to another side and cook for 10 minutes more.
4. Serve and enjoy.

Steak Fingers

Servings: 4
Cooking Time: 8 Minutes
Ingredients:
- 4 small beef cube steaks
- salt and pepper
- ½ cup flour
- oil for misting or cooking spray

Directions:
1. Cut cube steaks into 1-inch-wide strips.
2. Sprinkle lightly with salt and pepper to taste.
3. Roll in flour to coat all sides.
4. Spray air fryer basket with cooking spray or oil.
5. Place steak strips in air fryer basket in single layer, very close together but not touching. Spray top of steak strips with oil or cooking spray.
6. Cook at 390°F for 4minutes, turn strips over, and spray with oil or cooking spray.
7. Cook 4 more minutes and test with fork for doneness. Steak fingers should be crispy outside with no red juices inside. If needed, cook an additional 4 minutes or until well done.
8. Repeat steps 5 through 7 to cook remaining strips.

Marinated Rib Eye

Servings:4
Cooking Time: 10 Minutes
Ingredients:
- 1 pound rib eye steak
- ¼ cup soy sauce
- 1 tablespoon Worcestershire sauce
- 1 tablespoon granular brown erythritol
- 2 tablespoons olive oil
- ½ teaspoon salt
- ¼ teaspoon ground black pepper

Directions:
1. Place rib eye in a large sealable bowl or bag and pour in soy sauce, Worcestershire sauce, erythritol, and olive oil. Seal and let marinate 30 minutes in the refrigerator.
2. Remove rib eye from marinade, pat dry, and sprinkle on all sides with salt and pepper. Place rib eye into ungreased air fryer basket. Adjust the temperature to 400°F and set the timer for 10 minutes. Steak will be done when browned at the edges and has an internal temperature of 150°F for medium or 180°F for well-done. Serve warm.

Simple Lamb Chops

Servings:2
Cooking Time:6 Minutes
Ingredients:
- 4 lamb chops
- Salt and black pepper, to taste
- 1 tablespoon olive oil

Directions:
1. Preheat the Air fryer to 390°F and grease an Air fryer basket.
2. Mix the olive oil, salt, and black pepper in a large bowl and add chops.
3. Arrange the chops in the Air fryer basket and cook for about 6 minutes.
4. Dish out the lamb chops and serve hot.

Steak Bites And Spicy Dipping Sauce

Servings:4
Cooking Time: 8 Minutes
Ingredients:
- 2 pounds sirloin steak, cut into 2" cubes
- 2 teaspoons salt
- 1 teaspoon ground black pepper
- 1 teaspoon garlic powder
- ½ cup mayonnaise
- 2 tablespoons sriracha

Directions:
1. Preheat the air fryer to 400°F.
2. Sprinkle steak with salt, pepper, and garlic powder.
3. Place steak in the air fryer basket and cook 8 minutes, shaking the basket twice during cooking, until internal temperature reaches at least 160°F.
4. In a small bowl, combine mayonnaise and sriracha. Serve with steak bites for dipping.

Honey Mesquite Pork Chops

Servings: 2
Cooking Time: 10 Minutes
Ingredients:
- 2 tablespoons mesquite seasoning
- ¼ cup honey
- 1 tablespoon olive oil
- 1 tablespoon water
- freshly ground black pepper
- 2 bone-in center cut pork chops

Directions:

1. Whisk the mesquite seasoning, honey, olive oil, water and freshly ground black pepper together in a shallow glass dish. Pierce the chops all over and on both sides with a fork or meat tenderizer. Add the pork chops to the marinade and massage the marinade into the chops. Cover and marinate for 30 minutes.
2. Preheat the air fryer to 330°F.
3. Transfer the pork chops to the air fryer basket and pour half of the marinade over the chops, reserving the remaining marinade. Air-fry the pork chops for 6 minutes. Flip the pork chops over and pour the remaining marinade on top. Air-fry for an additional 3 minutes at 330°F. Then, increase the air fryer temperature to 400°F and air-fry the pork chops for an additional minute.
4. Transfer the pork chops to a serving plate, and let them rest for 5 minutes before serving. If you'd like a sauce for these chops, pour the cooked marinade from the bottom of the air fryer over the top.

London Broil

Servings:4
Cooking Time: 12 Minutes
Ingredients:
- 1 pound top round steak
- 1 tablespoon Worcestershire sauce
- ¼ cup soy sauce
- 2 cloves garlic, peeled and finely minced
- ½ teaspoon ground black pepper
- ½ teaspoon salt
- 2 tablespoons salted butter, melted

Directions:
1. Place steak in a large sealable bowl or bag. Pour in Worcestershire sauce and soy sauce, then add garlic, pepper, and salt. Toss to coat. Seal and place into refrigerator to let marinate 2 hours.
2. Remove steak from marinade and pat dry. Drizzle top side with butter, then place into ungreased air fryer basket. Adjust the temperature to 375°F and set the timer for 12 minutes, turning steak halfway through cooking. Steak will be done when browned at the edges and it has an internal temperature of 150°F for medium or 180°F for well-done.
3. Let steak rest on a large plate 10 minutes before slicing into thin pieces. Serve warm.

Sweet And Spicy Spare Ribs

Servings:6
Cooking Time: 30 Minutes
Ingredients:
- ¼ cup granular brown erythritol
- 2 teaspoons paprika
- 2 teaspoons chili powder
- 1 teaspoon garlic powder
- ½ teaspoon cayenne pepper
- 2 teaspoons salt
- 1 teaspoon ground black pepper
- 1 rack pork spare ribs

Directions:
1. In a small bowl, mix erythritol, paprika, chili powder, garlic powder, cayenne pepper, salt, and black pepper. Rub spice mix over ribs on both sides. Place ribs on ungreased aluminum foil sheet and wrap to cover.
2. Place ribs into ungreased air fryer basket. Adjust the temperature to 400°F and set the timer for 25 minutes.
3. When timer beeps, remove ribs from foil, then place back into air fryer basket to cook an additional 5 minutes, turning halfway through cooking. Ribs will be browned and have an internal temperature of at least 180°F when done. Serve warm.

Lamb Chops

Servings: 2
Cooking Time: 20 Minutes
Ingredients:
- 2 teaspoons oil
- ½ teaspoon ground rosemary
- ½ teaspoon lemon juice
- 1 pound lamb chops, approximately 1-inch thick
- salt and pepper
- cooking spray

Directions:
1. Mix the oil, rosemary, and lemon juice together and rub into all sides of the lamb chops. Season to taste with salt and pepper.
2. For best flavor, cover lamb chops and allow them to rest in the fridge for 20 minutes.
3. Spray air fryer basket with nonstick spray and place lamb chops in it.
4. Cook at 360°F for approximately 20minutes. This will cook chops to medium. The meat will be juicy but have no remaining pink. Cook for a minute or two longer for well done chops. For rare chops, stop cooking after about 12minutes and check for doneness.

Air Fried Steak

Servings: 2
Cooking Time: 10 Minutes
Ingredients:
- 2 sirloin steaks
- 2 tsp olive oil
- 2 tbsp steak seasoning
- Pepper
- Salt

Directions:
1. Preheat the air fryer to 350°F.
2. Coat steak with olive oil and season with steak seasoning, pepper, and salt.
3. Spray air fryer basket with cooking spray and place steak in the air fryer basket.
4. Cook for 10 minutes. Turn halfway through.
5. Slice and serve.

Spinach And Mushroom Steak Rolls

Servings:4
Cooking Time: 19 Minutes
Ingredients:
- ½ medium yellow onion, peeled and chopped
- ½ cup chopped baby bella mushrooms
- 1 cup chopped fresh spinach
- 1 pound flank steak
- 8 slices provolone cheese
- 1 teaspoon salt
- ½ teaspoon ground black pepper
- Cooking spray

Directions:
1. In a medium skillet over medium heat, sauté onion 2 minutes until fragrant and beginning to soften. Add mushrooms and spinach and continue cooking 5 more minutes until spinach is wilted and mushrooms are soft.
2. Preheat the air fryer to 400°F.
3. Carefully butterfly steak, leaving the two halves connected. Place slices of cheese on top of steak, then top with cooked vegetables.
4. Place steak so that the grain runs horizontally. Tightly roll up steak and secure it closed with eight evenly placed toothpicks or eight sections of butcher's twine.
5. Slice steak into four rolls. Spritz with cooking spray, then sprinkle with salt and pepper. Place in the air fryer basket and cook 12 minutes until steak is brown on the edges and internal temperature reaches at least 160°F for well-done. Serve.

Boneless Ribeyes

Servings: 2
Cooking Time: 10-15 Minutes
Ingredients:

- 2 8-ounce boneless ribeye steaks
- 4 teaspoons Worcestershire sauce
- ½ teaspoon garlic powder
- pepper
- 4 teaspoons extra virgin olive oil
- salt

Directions:

1. Season steaks on both sides with Worcestershire sauce. Use the back of a spoon to spread evenly.
2. Sprinkle both sides of steaks with garlic powder and coarsely ground black pepper to taste.
3. Drizzle both sides of steaks with olive oil, again using the back of a spoon to spread evenly over surfaces.
4. Allow steaks to marinate for 30minutes.
5. Place both steaks in air fryer basket and cook at 390°F for 5minutes.
6. Turn steaks over and cook until done: medium rare: additional 5 minutes, medium: additional 7 minutes, well done: additional 10 minutes.
7. Remove steaks from air fryer basket and let sit 5minutes. Salt to taste and serve.

Basil Pork

Servings: 4
Cooking Time: 25 Minutes
Ingredients:

- 4 pork chops
- A pinch of salt and black pepper
- 2 teaspoons basil, dried
- 2 tablespoons olive oil
- ½ teaspoon chili powder

Directions:

1. In a pan that fits your air fryer, mix all the ingredients, toss, introduce in the fryer and cook at 400°F for 25 minutes. Divide everything between plates and serve.

Beef Short Ribs

Servings:4
Cooking Time: 25 Minutes
Ingredients:

- 3 pounds beef short ribs
- 2 tablespoons olive oil
- 3 teaspoons salt
- 3 teaspoons ground black pepper
- ½ cup barbecue sauce

Directions:

1. Preheat the air fryer to 375°F.
2. Place short ribs in a large bowl. Drizzle with oil and sprinkle both sides with salt and pepper.
3. Place in the air fryer basket and cook 20 minutes. Remove from basket and brush with barbecue sauce. Return to the air fryer basket and cook 5 additional minutes until sauce is dark brown and internal temperature reaches at least 160°F. Serve warm.

Lamb Koftas Meatballs

Servings: 3
Cooking Time: 8 Minutes
Ingredients:

- 1 pound ground lamb
- 1 teaspoon ground cumin
- 1 teaspoon ground coriander
- 2 tablespoons chopped fresh mint
- 1 egg, beaten
- ½ teaspoon salt
- freshly ground black pepper

Directions:

1. Combine all ingredients in a bowl and mix together well. Divide the mixture into 10 portions. Roll each portion into a ball and then by cupping the meatball in your hand, shape it into an oval.
2. Preheat the air fryer to 400°F.
3. Air-fry the koftas for 8 minutes.
4. Serve warm with the cucumber-yogurt dip.

Fish And Seafood Recipes

Lemon-basil On Cod Filet

Servings:4
Cooking Time: 15 Minutes
Ingredients:

- ¼ cup olive oil
- 4 cod fillets
- A bunch of basil, torn
- Juice from 1 lemon, freshly squeezed
- Salt and pepper to taste

Directions:

1. Preheat the air fryer for 5 minutes.
2. Season the cod fillets with salt and pepper to taste. Place on lightly greased air fryer baking pan.
3. Mix the rest of the ingredients in a bowl and toss to combine. Pour over fish.
4. Cook for 15 minutes at 330°F.
5. Serve and enjoy.

Lobster Tails

Servings:4
Cooking Time: 10 Minutes
Ingredients:

- 4 lobster tails
- 2 tablespoons salted butter, melted
- 1 tablespoon finely minced garlic
- ¼ teaspoon salt
- ¼ teaspoon ground black pepper
- 2 tablespoons lemon juice

Directions:

1. Preheat the air fryer to 400°F.
2. Carefully cut open lobster tails with kitchen scissors and pull back the shell a little to expose the meat. Drizzle butter over each tail, then sprinkle with garlic, salt, and pepper.
3. Place tails in the air fryer basket and cook 10 minutes until lobster is firm and opaque and internal temperature reaches at least 145°F.
4. Drizzle lemon juice over lobster meat. Serve warm.

Potato-wrapped Salmon Fillets

Servings:3
Cooking Time: 8 Minutes
Ingredients:

- 1 Large 1-pound elongated yellow potato(es), peeled

- 3 6-ounce, 1½-inch-wide, quite thick skinless salmon fillets
- Olive oil spray
- ¼ teaspoon Table salt
- ¼ teaspoon Ground black pepper

Directions:

1. Preheat the air fryer to 400°F.
2. Use a vegetable peeler or mandoline to make long strips from the potato(es). You'll need anywhere from 8 to 12 strips per fillet, depending on the shape of the potato and of the salmon fillet.
3. Drape potato strips over a salmon fillet, overlapping the strips to create an even "crust." Tuck the potato strips under the fillet, overlapping the strips underneath to create as smooth a bottom as you can. Wrap the remaining fillet(s) in the same way.
4. Gently turn the fillets over. Generously coat the bottoms with olive oil spray. Turn them back seam side down and generously coat the tops with the oil spray. Sprinkle the salt and pepper over the wrapped fillets.
5. Use a nonstick-safe spatula to gently transfer the fillets seam side down to the basket. It helps to remove the basket from the machine and set it on your work surface (keeping in mind that the basket's hot). Leave as much air space as possible between the fillets. Air-fry undisturbed for 8 minutes, or until golden brown and crisp.
6. Use a nonstick-safe spatula to gently transfer the fillets to serving plates. Cool for a couple of minutes before serving.

5-minute Shrimp

Servings:4
Cooking Time: 5 Minutes
Ingredients:

- 1 pound medium shrimp, peeled and deveined
- 2 tablespoons salted butter, melted
- ¼ teaspoon salt
- ¼ teaspoon ground black pepper

Directions:

1. In a large bowl, toss shrimp in butter, then sprinkle with salt and pepper.
2. Place shrimp into ungreased air fryer basket. Adjust the temperature to 400°F and set the timer for 5 minutes, shaking the basket halfway through cooking. Shrimp will be opaque and pink when done. Serve warm.

Nacho Chips Crusted Prawns

Servings:2
Cooking Time: 8 Minutes
Ingredients:
- ¾ pound prawns, peeled and deveined
- 1 large egg
- 5 ounces Nacho flavored chips, finely crushed

Directions:
1. In a shallow bowl, beat the egg.
2. In another bowl, place the nacho chips
3. Dip each prawn into the beaten egg and then, coat with the crushed nacho chips.
4. Set the temperature of air fryer to 350°F. Grease an air fryer basket.
5. Arrange prawns into the prepared air fryer basket.
6. Air fry for about 8 minutes.
7. Remove from air fryer and transfer the prawns onto serving plates.
8. Serve hot.

Honey-glazed Salmon

Servings:4
Cooking Time: 30 Minutes
Ingredients:
- 2 tablespoons soy sauce
- 1 teaspoon sriracha
- ½ teaspoon minced garlic
- 4 skin-on salmon fillets
- 2 teaspoons honey

Directions:
1. In a large bowl, whisk together soy sauce, sriracha, and garlic. Place salmon in bowl. Cover and let marinate in refrigerator at least 20 minutes.
2. Preheat the air fryer to 375°F.
3. Place salmon in the air fryer basket and cook 8 minutes. Open air fryer and brush honey on salmon. Continue cooking 2 more minutes until salmon flakes easily and internal temperature reaches at least 145°F. Serve warm.

Garlic Lemon Scallops

Servings:4
Cooking Time: 10 Minutes
Ingredients:
- 4 tablespoons salted butter, melted
- 4 teaspoons peeled and finely minced garlic
- ½ small lemon, zested and juiced
- 8 sea scallops, cleaned and patted dry
- ¼ teaspoon salt
- ¼ teaspoon ground black pepper

Directions:
1. In a small bowl, mix butter, garlic, lemon zest, and lemon juice. Place scallops in an ungreased 6" round nonstick baking dish. Pour butter mixture over scallops, then sprinkle with salt and pepper.
2. Place dish into air fryer basket. Adjust the temperature to 360°F and set the timer for 10 minutes. Scallops will be opaque and firm, and have an internal temperature of 130°F when done. Serve warm.

Very Easy Lime-garlic Shrimps

Servings:1
Cooking Time: 6 Minutes
Ingredients:
- 1 clove of garlic, minced
- 1 cup raw shrimps
- 1 lime, juiced and zested
- Salt and pepper to taste

Directions:
1. In a mixing bowl, combine all Ingredients and give a good stir.
2. Preheat the air fryer to 390°F.
3. Skewer the shrimps onto the metal skewers that come with the double layer rack accessory.
4. Place on the rack and cook for 6 minutes.

Tilapia Teriyaki

Servings: 3
Cooking Time: 10 Minutes
Ingredients:
- 4 tablespoons teriyaki sauce
- 1 tablespoon pineapple juice
- 1 pound tilapia fillets
- cooking spray
- 6 ounces frozen mixed peppers with onions, thawed and drained
- 2 cups cooked rice

Directions:
1. Mix the teriyaki sauce and pineapple juice together in a small bowl.
2. Split tilapia fillets down the center lengthwise.
3. Brush all sides of fish with the sauce, spray air fryer basket with nonstick cooking spray, and place fish in the basket.
4. Stir the peppers and onions into the remaining sauce and spoon over the fish. Save any leftover sauce for drizzling over the fish when serving.
5. Cook at 360°F for 10 minutes, until fish flakes easily with a fork and is done in center.
6. Divide into 3 or 4 servings and serve each with approximately ½ cup cooked rice.

Salmon Patties

Servings:4

Cooking Time: 12 Minutes

Ingredients:

- 1 pouch cooked salmon
- 6 tablespoons panko bread crumbs
- ½ cup mayonnaise
- 2 teaspoons Old Bay Seasoning

Directions:

1. Preheat the air fryer to 350°F.

2. In a large bowl, combine all ingredients.

3. Divide mixture into four equal portions. Using your hands, form into patties and spritz with cooking spray.

4. Place in the air fryer basket and cook 12 minutes, turning halfway through cooking time, until brown and firm. Serve warm.

Air Fried Calamari

Servings:3

Cooking Time: 30 Minutes

Ingredients:

- ½ cup cornmeal or cornstarch
- 2 large eggs, beaten
- 2 mashed garlic cloves
- 1 cup breadcrumbs
- lemon juice

Directions:

1. Coat calamari with the cornmeal. The first mixture is prepared by mixing the eggs and garlic. Dip the calamari in the eggs' mixture. Then dip them in the breadcrumbs. Put the rings in the fridge for 2 hours.

2. Then, line them in the air fryer and add oil generously. Fry for 10 to 13 minutes at 390°F, shaking once halfway through. Serve with garlic mayonnaise and top with lemon juice.

Fish-in-chips

Servings:4

Cooking Time: 11 Minutes

Ingredients:

- 1 cup All-purpose flour or potato starch
- 2 Large egg(s), well beaten
- 1½ cups Crushed plain potato chips, preferably thick-cut or ruffled (gluten-free, if a concern)
- 4 4-ounce skinless cod fillets

Directions:

1. Preheat the air fryer to 400°F.

2. Set up and fill three shallow soup plates or small pie plates on your counter: one for the flour, one for the beaten egg(s), and one for the crushed potato chips.

3. Dip a piece of cod in the flour, turning it to coat on all sides, even the ends and sides. Gently shake off any excess flour, then dip it in the beaten egg(s). Gently turn to coat it on all sides, then let any excess egg slip back into the rest. Set the fillet in the crushed potato chips and turn several times and onto all sides, pressing gently to coat the fish. Dip it back in the egg(s), coating all sides but taking care that the coating doesn't slip off; then dip it back in the potato chips for a thick, even coating. Set it aside and coat more fillets in the same way.

4. When the machine is at temperature, set the fillets in the basket with as much air space between them as possible. Air-fry undisturbed for 11 minutes, until golden brown and firm but not hard.

5. Use kitchen tongs to transfer the fillets to a wire rack. Cool for just a minute or two before serving.

Great Cat Fish

Servings:4

Cooking Time: 25 Minutes

Ingredients:

- ¼ cup seasoned fish fry
- 1 tbsp olive oil
- 1 tbsp parsley, chopped

Directions:

1. Preheat your air fryer to 400°F, and add seasoned fish fry, and fillets in a large Ziploc bag; massage well to coat. Place the fillets in your air fryer's cooking basket and cook for 10 minutes. Flip the fish and cook for 2-3 more minutes. Top with parsley and serve.

Lemon Butter Cod

Servings:4

Cooking Time: 12 Minutes

Ingredients:

- 4 cod fillets
- 2 tablespoons salted butter, melted
- 1 teaspoon Old Bay Seasoning
- ½ medium lemon, cut into 4 slices

Directions:

1. Place cod fillets into an ungreased 6" round nonstick baking dish. Brush tops of fillets with butter and sprinkle with Old Bay Seasoning. Lay 1 lemon slice on each fillet.

2. Cover dish with aluminum foil and place into air fryer basket. Adjust the temperature to 350°F and set the timer for 12 minutes, turning fillets halfway through cooking. Fish will be opaque and have an internal temperature of at least 145°F when done. Serve warm.

Ham Tilapia

Servings: 4
Cooking Time: 10 Minutes
Ingredients:
- 16 oz tilapia fillet
- 4 ham slices
- 1 teaspoon sunflower oil
- ½ teaspoon salt
- 1 teaspoon dried rosemary

Directions:
1. Cut the tilapia on 4 servings. Sprinkle every fish serving with salt, dried rosemary, and sunflower oil. Then carefully wrap the fish fillets in the ham slices and secure with toothpicks. Preheat the air fryer to 400°F. Put the wrapped tilapia in the air fryer basket in one layer and cook them for 10 minutes. Gently flip the fish on another side after 5 minutes of cooking.

Coriander Cod And Green Beans

Servings: 4
Cooking Time: 15 Minutes
Ingredients:
- 12 oz cod fillet
- ½ cup green beans, trimmed and halved
- 1 tablespoon avocado oil
- 1 teaspoon salt
- 1 teaspoon ground coriander

Directions:
1. Cut the cod fillet on 4 servings and sprinkle every serving with salt and ground coriander. After this, place the fish on 4 foil squares. Top them with green beans and avocado oil and wrap them into parcels. Preheat the air fryer to 400°F. Place the cod parcels in the air fryer and cook them for 15 minutes.

Fish Sticks

Servings: 4
Cooking Time: 20 Minutes
Ingredients:
- 1 lb. tilapia fillets, cut into strips
- 1 large egg, beaten
- 2 tsp. Old Bay seasoning
- 1 tbsp. olive oil
- 1 cup friendly bread crumbs

Directions:
1. Pre-heat the Air Fryer at 400°F.
2. In a shallow dish, combine together the bread crumbs, Old Bay, and oil. Put the egg in a small bowl.

3. Dredge the fish sticks in the egg. Cover them with bread crumbs and put them in the fryer's basket.
4. Cook the fish for 10 minutes or until they turn golden brown.
5. Serve hot.

Outrageous Crispy Fried Salmon Skin

Servings:4
Cooking Time: 10 Minutes
Ingredients:
- ½ pound salmon skin, patted dry
- 4 tablespoons coconut oil
- Salt and pepper to taste

Directions:
1. Preheat the air fryer for 5 minutes.
2. In a large bowl, combine everything and mix well.
3. Place in the fryer basket and close.
4. Cook for 10 minutes at 400°F.
5. Halfway through the cooking time, give a good shake to evenly cook the skin.

Easy-peasy Shrimp

Servings:2
Cooking Time: 15 Minutes
Ingredients:
- 1 lb tail-on shrimp, deveined
- 2 tbsp butter, melted
- 1 tbsp lemon juice
- 1 tbsp dill, chopped

Directions:
1. Preheat air fryer to 350°F. Combine shrimp and butter in a bowl. Place shrimp in the greased frying basket and Air Fry for 6 minutes, flipping once. Squeeze lemon juice over and top with dill. Serve hot.

Potato-crusted Cod

Servings:4
Cooking Time: 15 Minutes
Ingredients:
- 4 boneless, skinless cod fillets
- 2 tablespoons olive oil
- ½ teaspoon salt, divided
- 1 teaspoon dried dill
- 2 cups mashed potato flakes

Directions:
1. Preheat the air fryer to 350°F.
2. Place cod fillets on a work surface and brush with oil. Sprinkle with ¼ teaspoon salt and dill.
3. In a large bowl, combine mashed potato flakes with remaining salt.
4. Roll each fillet in the potato mixture and spritz with cooking spray.
5. Place in the air fryer basket and cook 15 minutes, turning halfway through cooking time. Cod will be golden brown and have an internal temperature of at least 145°F when done. Serve warm.

Catalan Sardines With Romesco Sauce

Servings:2
Cooking Time: 15 Minutes
Ingredients:
- 2 cans skinless, boneless sardines in oil, drained
- ½ cup warmed romesco sauce
- ½ cup bread crumbs

Directions:
1. Preheat air fryer to 350°F. In a shallow dish, add bread crumbs. Roll in sardines to coat. Place sardines in the greased frying basket and Air Fry for 6 minutes, turning once. Serve with romesco sauce.

Lime Flaming Halibut

Servings:2
Cooking Time: 20 Minutes
Ingredients:
- 2 tbsp butter, melted
- ½ tsp chili powder
- ½ cup bread crumbs
- 2 halibut fillets

Directions:
1. Preheat air fryer to 350°F. In a bowl, mix the butter, chili powder and bread crumbs. Press mixture onto tops of halibut fillets. Place halibut in the greased frying basket and Air Fry for 10 minutes or until the fish is opaque and flake easily with a fork. Serve right away.

Teriyaki Salmon

Servings:4
Cooking Time: 27 Minutes
Ingredients:
- ½ cup teriyaki sauce
- ¼ teaspoon salt
- 1 teaspoon ground ginger
- ½ teaspoon garlic powder
- 4 boneless, skinless salmon fillets
- 2 tablespoons toasted sesame seeds

Directions:
1. In a large bowl, whisk teriyaki sauce, salt, ginger, and garlic powder. Add salmon to the bowl, being sure to coat each side with marinade. Cover and let marinate in refrigerator 15 minutes.
2. Preheat the air fryer to 375°F.
3. Spritz fillets with cooking spray and place in the air fryer basket. Cook 12 minutes, turning halfway through cooking time, until glaze has caramelized to a dark brown color, salmon flakes easily, and internal temperature reaches at least 145°F. Sprinkle sesame seeds on salmon and serve warm.

Restaurant-style Flounder Cutlets

Servings: 2
Cooking Time: 15 Minutes
Ingredients:
- 1 egg
- 1 cup Pecorino Romano cheese, grated
- Sea salt and white pepper, to taste
- 1/2 teaspoon cayenne pepper
- 1 teaspoon dried parsley flakes
- 2 flounder fillets

Directions:
1. To make a breading station, whisk the egg until frothy.
2. In another bowl, mix Pecorino Romano cheese, and spices.
3. Dip the fish in the egg mixture and turn to coat evenly; then, dredge in the cracker crumb mixture, turning a couple of times to coat evenly.
4. Cook in the preheated Air Fryer at 390°F for 5 minutes; turn them over and cook another 5 minutes. Enjoy!

Coconut Shrimp

Servings:4
Cooking Time: 10 Minutes
Ingredients:
- 1 cup all-purpose flour
- 1 teaspoon salt
- 2 large eggs
- ½ cup panko bread crumbs
- 1 cup shredded unsweetened coconut flakes
- 1 pound large shrimp, peeled and deveined
- Cooking spray

Directions:
1. Preheat the air fryer to 375°F.
2. In a medium bowl, mix flour and salt. In a separate medium bowl, whisk eggs. In a third medium bowl, mix bread crumbs and coconut flakes.
3. Dredge shrimp first in flour mixture, shaking off excess, then in eggs, letting any additional egg drip off, and finally in bread crumb mixture. Spritz with cooking spray.
4. Place shrimp in the air fryer basket. Cook 10 minutes, turning and spritzing opposite side with cooking spray halfway through cooking, until insides are pearly white and opaque and internal temperature reaches at least 145°F. Serve warm.

Chili Lime Shrimp

Servings:4
Cooking Time: 5 Minutes
Ingredients:
- 1 pound medium shrimp, peeled and deveined
- 1 tablespoon salted butter, melted
- 2 teaspoons chili powder
- ¼ teaspoon garlic powder
- ¼ teaspoon salt
- ¼ teaspoon ground black pepper
- ½ small lime, zested and juiced, divided

Directions:
1. In a medium bowl, toss shrimp with butter, then sprinkle with chili powder, garlic powder, salt, pepper, and lime zest.
2. Place shrimp into ungreased air fryer basket. Adjust the temperature to 400°F and set the timer for 5 minutes. Shrimp will be firm and form a "C" shape when done.
3. Transfer shrimp to a large serving dish and drizzle with lime juice. Serve warm.

Maple Balsamic Glazed Salmon

Servings: 4
Cooking Time: 10 Minutes
Ingredients:
- 4 fillets of salmon
- salt and freshly ground black pepper
- vegetable oil
- ¼ cup pure maple syrup
- 3 tablespoons balsamic vinegar
- 1 teaspoon Dijon mustard

Directions:
1. Preheat the air fryer to 400°F.
2. Season the salmon well with salt and freshly ground black pepper. Spray or brush the bottom of the air fryer basket with vegetable oil and place the salmon fillets inside. Air-fry the salmon for 5 minutes.
3. While the salmon is air-frying, combine the maple syrup, balsamic vinegar and Dijon mustard in a small saucepan over medium heat and stir to blend well. Let the mixture simmer while the fish is cooking. It should start to thicken slightly, but keep your eye on it so it doesn't burn.
4. Brush the glaze on the salmon fillets and air-fry for an additional 5 minutes. The salmon should feel firm to the touch when finished and the glaze should be nicely browned on top. Brush a little more glaze on top before removing and serving with rice and vegetables, or a nice green salad.

Tuna-stuffed Tomatoes

Servings:2
Cooking Time: 5 Minutes
Ingredients:
- 2 medium beefsteak tomatoes, tops removed, seeded, membranes removed
- 2 pouches tuna packed in water, drained
- 1 medium stalk celery, trimmed and chopped
- 2 tablespoons mayonnaise
- ¼ teaspoon salt
- ¼ teaspoon ground black pepper
- 2 teaspoons coconut oil
- ¼ cup shredded mild Cheddar cheese

Directions:
1. Scoop pulp out of each tomato, leaving ½" shell.
2. In a medium bowl, mix tuna, celery, mayonnaise, salt, and pepper. Drizzle with coconut oil. Spoon ½ mixture into each tomato and top each with 2 tablespoons Cheddar.
3. Place tomatoes into ungreased air fryer basket. Adjust the temperature to 320°F and set the timer for 5 minutes. Cheese will be melted when done. Serve warm.

Simple Salmon

Servings:2
Cooking Time:10 Minutes
Ingredients:
- 2 salmon fillets
- Salt and black pepper, as required
- 1 tablespoon olive oil

Directions:
1. Preheat the Air fryer to 390°F and grease an Air fryer basket.
2. Season each salmon fillet with salt and black pepper and drizzle with olive oil.
3. Arrange salmon fillets into the Air fryer basket and cook for about 10 minutes.
4. Remove from the Air fryer and dish out the salmon fillets onto the serving plates.

Garlic And Dill Salmon

Servings: 2
Cooking Time: 8 Minutes
Ingredients:
- 12 ounces salmon filets with skin
- 2 tablespoons melted butter
- 1 tablespoon extra-virgin olive oil
- 2 garlic cloves, minced
- 1 tablespoon fresh dill
- ½ teaspoon sea salt
- ½ lemon

Directions:
1. Pat the salmon dry with paper towels.
2. In a small bowl, mix together the melted butter, olive oil, garlic, and dill.
3. Sprinkle the top of the salmon with sea salt. Brush all sides of the salmon with the garlic and dill butter.
4. Preheat the air fryer to 350°F.
5. Place the salmon, skin side down, in the air fryer basket. Cook for 6 to 8 minutes, or until the fish flakes in the center.
6. Remove the salmon and plate on a serving platter. Squeeze fresh lemon over the top of the salmon. Serve immediately.

Crunchy Coconut Shrimp

Servings:2
Cooking Time: 8 Minutes
Ingredients:
- 8 ounces jumbo shrimp, peeled and deveined
- 2 tablespoons salted butter, melted
- ½ teaspoon Old Bay Seasoning
- ¼ cup unsweetened shredded coconut
- ¼ cup coconut flour

Directions:
1. In a large bowl, toss shrimp in butter and Old Bay Seasoning.
2. In a medium bowl, combine shredded coconut with coconut flour. Coat each piece of shrimp in coconut mixture.
3. Place shrimp into ungreased air fryer basket. Adjust the temperature to 400°F and set the timer for 8 minutes, gently turning shrimp halfway through cooking. Shrimp will be pink and C-shaped when done. Serve warm.

Crispy Sweet-and-sour Cod Fillets

Servings:3
Cooking Time: 12 Minutes
Ingredients:
- 1½ cups Plain panko bread crumbs (gluten-free, if a concern)
- 2 tablespoons Regular or low-fat mayonnaise (not fat-free; gluten-free, if a concern)
- ¼ cup Sweet pickle relish
- 3 4- to 5-ounce skinless cod fillets

Directions:
1. Preheat the air fryer to 400°F.
2. Pour the bread crumbs into a shallow soup plate or a small pie plate. Mix the mayonnaise and relish in a small bowl until well combined. Smear this mixture all over the cod fillets. Set them in the crumbs and turn until evenly coated on all sides, even on the ends.
3. Set the coated cod fillets in the basket with as much air space between them as possible. They should not touch. Air-fry undisturbed for 12 minutes, or until browned and crisp.
4. Use a nonstick-safe spatula to transfer the cod pieces to a wire rack. Cool for only a minute or two before serving hot.

Spicy Fish Taco Bowl

Servings:4
Cooking Time: 12 Minutes
Ingredients:

- ½ teaspoon salt
- ¼ teaspoon garlic powder
- ¼ teaspoon ground cumin
- 4 cod fillets
- 4 cups finely shredded green cabbage
- ⅓ cup mayonnaise
- ¼ teaspoon ground black pepper
- ¼ cup chopped pickled jalapeños

Directions:

1. Sprinkle salt, garlic powder, and cumin over cod and place into ungreased air fryer basket. Adjust the temperature to 350°F and set the timer for 12 minutes, turning fillets halfway through cooking. Cod will flake easily and have an internal temperature of at least 145°F when done.

2. In a large bowl, toss cabbage with mayonnaise, pepper, and jalapeños until fully coated. Serve cod warm over cabbage slaw on four medium plates.

Mahi-mahi "burrito" Fillets

Servings:3
Cooking Time: 10 Minutes
Ingredients:

- 1 Large egg white
- 1½ cups Crushed corn tortilla chips (gluten-free, if a concern)
- 1 tablespoon Chile powder
- 3 5-ounce skinless mahi-mahi fillets
- 6 tablespoons Canned refried beans
- Vegetable oil spray

Directions:

1. Preheat the air fryer to 400°F.

2. Set up and fill two shallow soup plates or small pie plates on your counter: one with the egg white, beaten until foamy; and one with the crushed tortilla chips.

3. Gently rub ½ teaspoon chile powder on each side of each fillet.

4. Spread 1 tablespoon refried beans over both sides and the edges of a fillet. Dip the fillet in the egg white, turning to coat it on both sides. Let any excess egg white slip back into the rest, then set the fillet in the crushed tortilla chips. Turn several times, pressing gently to coat it evenly. Coat the fillet on all sides with the vegetable oil spray, then set it aside. Prepare the remaining fillet(s) in the same way.

5. When the machine is at temperature, set the fillets in the basket with as much air space between them as possible. Air-fry undisturbed for 10 minutes, or until crisp and browned.

6. Use a nonstick-safe spatula to transfer the fillets to a serving platter or plates. Cool for only a minute or so, then serve hot.

Lemon And Thyme Sea Bass

Servings: 3
Cooking Time: 15 Minutes
Ingredients:

- 8 oz sea bass, trimmed, peeled
- 4 lemon slices
- 1 tablespoon thyme
- 2 teaspoons sesame oil
- 1 teaspoon salt

Directions:

1. Fill the sea bass with lemon slices and rub with thyme, salt, and sesame oil. Then preheat the air fryer to 385°F and put the fish in the air fryer basket. Cook it for 12 minutes. Then flip the fish on another side and cook it for 3 minutes more.

Swordfish With Capers And Tomatoes

Servings: 2
Cooking Time: 10 Minutes
Ingredients:

- 2 1-inch thick swordfish steaks
- A pinch of salt and black pepper
- 30 ounces tomatoes, chopped
- 2 tablespoons capers, drained
- 1 tablespoon red vinegar
- 2 tablespoons oregano, chopped

Directions:

1. In a pan that fits the air fryer, combine all the ingredients, toss, put the pan in the fryer and cook at 390°F for 10 minutes, flipping the fish halfway. Divide the mix between plates and serve.

Sea Scallops

Servings: 4
Cooking Time: 8 Minutes
Ingredients:

- 1½ pounds sea scallops
- salt and pepper
- 2 eggs
- ½ cup flour
- ½ cup plain breadcrumbs
- oil for misting or cooking spray

Directions:

1. Rinse scallops and remove the tough side muscle. Sprinkle to taste with salt and pepper.
2. Beat eggs together in a shallow dish. Place flour in a second shallow dish and breadcrumbs in a third.
3. Preheat air fryer to 390°F.
4. Dip scallops in flour, then eggs, and then roll in breadcrumbs. Mist with oil or cooking spray.
5. Place scallops in air fryer basket in a single layer, leaving some space between. You should be able to cook about a dozen at a time.
6. Cook at 390°F for 8 minutes, watching carefully so as not to overcook. Scallops are done when they turn opaque all the way through. They will feel slightly firm when pressed with tines of a fork.
7. Repeat step 6 to cook remaining scallops.

Butternut Squash–wrapped Halibut Fillets

Servings:3
Cooking Time: 11 Minutes
Ingredients:

- 15 Long spiralized peeled and seeded butternut squash strands
- 3 5- to 6-ounce skinless halibut fillets
- 3 tablespoons Butter, melted
- ¾ teaspoon Mild paprika
- ¾ teaspoon Table salt
- ¾ teaspoon Ground black pepper

Directions:

1. Preheat the air fryer to 375°F .
2. Hold 5 long butternut squash strands together and wrap them around a fillet. Set it aside and wrap any remaining fillet(s).
3. Mix the melted butter, paprika, salt, and pepper in a small bowl. Brush this mixture over the squash-wrapped fillets on all sides.
4. When the machine is at temperature, set the fillets in the basket with as much air space between them as possible. Air-fry undisturbed for 10 minutes, or until the squash strands have browned but not burned. If the machine is at 360°F, you may need to add 1 minute

to the cooking time. In any event, watch the fish carefully after the 8-minute mark.
5. Use a nonstick-safe spatula to gently transfer the fillets to a serving platter or plates. Cool for only a minute or so before serving.

Air Fried Cod With Basil Vinaigrette

Servings:4
Cooking Time: 15 Minutes
Ingredients:

- ¼ cup olive oil
- 4 cod fillets
- A bunch of basil, torn
- Juice from 1 lemon, freshly squeezed
- Salt and pepper to taste

Directions:

1. Preheat the air fryer for 5 minutes.
2. Season the cod fillets with salt and pepper to taste.
3. Place in the air fryer and cook for 15 minutes at 350°F.
4. Meanwhile, mix the rest of the ingredients in a bowl and toss to combine.
5. Serve the air fried cod with the basil vinaigrette.

Miso-rubbed Salmon Fillets

Servings:3
Cooking Time: 5 Minutes
Ingredients:

- ¼ cup White (shiro) miso paste (usually made from rice and soy beans)
- 1½ tablespoons Mirin or a substitute
- 2½ teaspoons Unseasoned rice vinegar
- Vegetable oil spray
- 3 6-ounce skin-on salmon fillets

Directions:

1. Preheat the air fryer to 400°F.
2. Mix the miso, mirin, and vinegar in a small bowl until uniform.
3. Remove the basket from the machine. Generously spray the skin side of each fillet. Pick them up one by one with a nonstick-safe spatula and set them in the basket skin side down with as much air space between them as possible. Coat the top of each fillet with the miso mixture, dividing it evenly between them.
4. Return the basket to the machine. Air-fry undisturbed for 5 minutes, or until lightly browned and firm.
5. Use a nonstick-safe spatula to transfer the fillets to serving plates. Cool for only a minute or so before serving.

Fish Taco Bowl

Servings:4
Cooking Time: 12 Minutes
Ingredients:

- 2 cups finely shredded cabbage
- ½ cup mayonnaise
- Juice of 1 medium lime, divided
- 4 boneless, skinless tilapia fillets
- 2 teaspoons chili powder
- 1 teaspoon salt
- ½ teaspoon ground black pepper

Directions:

1. In a large bowl, mix cabbage, mayonnaise, and half of lime juice to make a slaw. Cover and refrigerate while the fish cooks.
2. Preheat the air fryer to 400°F.
3. Sprinkle tilapia with chili powder, salt, and pepper. Spritz each side with cooking spray.
4. Place fillets in the air fryer basket and cook 12 minutes, turning halfway through cooking time, until fish is opaque, flakes easily, and reaches an internal temperature of 145°F.
5. Allow fish to cool 5 minutes before chopping into bite-sized pieces. To serve, place ½ cup slaw into each bowl and top with one-fourth of fish. Squeeze remaining lime juice over fish. Serve warm.

Better Fish Sticks

Servings:3
Cooking Time: 8 Minutes
Ingredients:

- ¾ cup Seasoned Italian-style dried bread crumbs (gluten-free, if a concern)
- 3 tablespoons (about ½ ounce) Finely grated Parmesan cheese
- 10 ounces Skinless cod fillets, cut lengthwise into 1-inch-wide pieces
- 3 tablespoons Regular or low-fat mayonnaise (not fat-free; gluten-free, if a concern)
- Vegetable oil spray

Directions:

1. Preheat the air fryer to 400°F.
2. Mix the bread crumbs and grated Parmesan in a shallow soup bowl or a small pie plate.
3. Smear the fish fillet sticks completely with the mayonnaise, then dip them one by one in the bread-crumb mixture, turning and pressing gently to make an even and thorough coating. Coat each stick on all sides with vegetable oil spray.

4. Set the fish sticks in the basket with at least ¼ inch between them. Air-fry undisturbed for 8 minutes, or until golden brown and crisp.
5. Use a nonstick-safe spatula to gently transfer them from the basket to a wire rack. Cool for only a minute or two before serving.

Catfish Nuggets

Servings: 4
Cooking Time: 7 Minutes Per Batch
Ingredients:

- 2 medium catfish fillets, cut in chunks
- salt and pepper
- 2 eggs
- 2 tablespoons skim milk
- ½ cup cornstarch
- 1 cup panko breadcrumbs, crushed
- oil for misting or cooking spray

Directions:

1. Season catfish chunks with salt and pepper to your liking.
2. Beat together eggs and milk in a small bowl.
3. Place cornstarch in a second small bowl.
4. Place breadcrumbs in a third small bowl.
5. Dip catfish chunks in cornstarch, dip in egg wash, shake off excess, then roll in breadcrumbs.
6. Spray all sides of catfish chunks with oil or cooking spray.
7. Place chunks in air fryer basket in a single layer, leaving space between for air circulation.
8. Cook at 390°F for 4minutes, turn, and cook an additional 3 minutes, until fish flakes easily and outside is crispy brown.
9. Repeat steps 7 and 8 to cook remaining catfish nuggets.

Perfect Soft-shelled Crabs

Servings:2
Cooking Time: 12 Minutes
Ingredients:
- ½ cup All-purpose flour
- 1 tablespoon Old Bay seasoning
- 1 Large egg(s), well beaten
- 1 cup Ground oyster crackers
- 2 2½-ounce cleaned soft-shelled crab(s), about 4 inches across
- Vegetable oil spray

Directions:
1. Preheat the air fryer to 375°F.
2. Set up and fill three shallow soup plates or small pie plates on your counter: one for the flour, whisked with the Old Bay until well combined; one for the beaten egg(s); and one for the cracker crumbs.
3. Set a soft-shelled crab in the flour mixture and turn to coat evenly and well on all sides, even inside the legs. Dip the crab into the egg(s) and coat well, turning at least once, again getting some of the egg between the legs. Let any excess egg slip back into the rest, then set the crab in the cracker crumbs. Turn several times, pressing very gently to get the crab evenly coated with crumbs, even between the legs. Generously coat the crab on all sides with vegetable oil spray. Set it aside if you're making more than one and coat these in the same way.
4. Set the crab(s) in the basket with as much air space between them as possible. They may overlap slightly, particularly at the ends of their legs, depending on the basket's size. Air-fry undisturbed for 12 minutes, or until very crisp and golden brown. If the machine is at 390°F, the crabs may be done in only 10 minutes.
5. Use kitchen tongs to gently transfer the crab(s) to a wire rack. Cool for a couple of minutes before serving.

Shrimp Al Pesto

Servings: 4
Cooking Time: 10 Minutes
Ingredients:
- 1 lb peeled shrimp, deveined
- ¼ cup pesto sauce
- 1 lime, sliced
- 2 cups cooked farro

Directions:
1. Preheat air fryer to 360°F. Coat the shrimp with the pesto sauce in a bowl. Put the shrimp in a single layer in the frying basket. Put the lime slices over the shrimp and Roast for 5 minutes. Remove lime and discard. Serve the shrimp over a bed of farro pilaf. Enjoy!

Quick And Easy Shrimp

Servings:2
Cooking Time:5 Minutes
Ingredients:
- ½ pound tiger shrimp
- 1 tablespoon olive oil
- ½ teaspoon old bay seasoning
- ¼ teaspoon smoked paprika
- ¼ teaspoon cayenne pepper
- Salt, to taste

Directions:
1. Preheat the Air fryer to 390°F and grease an Air fryer basket.
2. Mix all the ingredients in a large bowl until well combined.
3. Place the shrimps in the Air fryer basket and cook for about 5 minutes.
4. Dish out and serve warm.

Stevia Cod

Servings: 4
Cooking Time: 14 Minutes
Ingredients:
- 1/3 cup stevia
- 2 tablespoons coconut aminos
- 4 cod fillets, boneless
- A pinch of salt and black pepper

Directions:
1. In a pan that fits the air fryer, combine all the ingredients and toss gently. Introduce the pan in the fryer and cook at 350°F for 14 minutes, flipping the fish halfway. Divide everything between plates and serve.

Lime Bay Scallops

Servings:4
Cooking Time: 10 Minutes
Ingredients:
- 2 tbsp butter, melted
- 1 lime, juiced
- ¼ tsp salt
- 1 lb bay scallops
- 2 tbsp chopped cilantro

Directions:
1. Preheat air fryer to 350°F. Combine all ingredients in a bowl, except for the cilantro. Place scallops in the frying basket and Air Fry for 5 minutes, tossing once. Serve immediately topped with cilantro.

Garlic-lemon Scallops

Servings:4
Cooking Time: 12 Minutes
Ingredients:
- ¼ teaspoon salt
- ¼ teaspoon ground black pepper
- 8 sea scallops, rinsed and patted dry
- 4 tablespoons salted butter, melted
- 4 teaspoons finely minced garlic
- Zest and juice of ½ small lemon

Directions:
1. Preheat the air fryer to 375°F.
2. Sprinkle salt and pepper evenly over scallops. Spritz scallops lightly with cooking spray. Place in the air fryer basket in a single layer and cook 12 minutes, turning halfway through cooking time, until scallops are opaque and firm and internal temperature reaches at least 130°F.
3. While scallops are cooking, in a small bowl, mix butter, garlic, lemon zest, and juice. Set aside.
4. When scallops are done, drizzle with garlic–lemon butter. Serve warm.

Miso Fish

Servings: 2
Cooking Time: 10 Minutes
Ingredients:
- 2 cod fish fillets
- 1 tbsp garlic, chopped
- 2 tsp swerve
- 2 tbsp miso

Directions:
1. Add all ingredients to the zip-lock bag. Shake well place in the refrigerator for overnight.
2. Place marinated fish fillets into the air fryer basket and cook at 350°F for 10 minutes.
3. Serve and enjoy.

Poultry Recipes

Chicken Gruyere

Servings:4
Cooking Time: 20 Minutes
Ingredients:
- ¼ cup Gruyere cheese, grated
- 1 pound chicken breasts, boneless, skinless
- ½ cup flour
- 2 eggs, beaten
- Sea salt and black pepper to taste
- 4 lemon slices
- Cooking spray

Directions:
1. Preheat your Air Fryer to 370°F. Spray the air fryer basket with cooking spray.
2. Mix the breadcrumbs with Gruyere cheese in a bowl, pour the eggs in another bowl, and the flour in a third bowl. Toss the chicken in the flour, then in the eggs, and then in the breadcrumb mixture. Place in the fryer basket, close and cook for 12 minutes. At the 6-minute mark, turn the chicken over. Once golden brown, remove onto a serving plate and serve topped with lemon slices.

Herb-marinated Chicken

Servings: 4
Cooking Time: 25 Minutes
Ingredients:
- 4 chicken breasts
- 2 tsp rosemary, minced
- 2 tsp thyme, minced
- Salt and pepper to taste
- ½ cup chopped cilantro
- 1 lime, juiced
- Cooking spray

Directions:
1. Place chicken in a resealable bag. Add rosemary, thyme, salt, pepper, cilantro, and lime juice. Seal the bag and toss to coat, then place in the refrigerator for 2 hours.
2. Preheat air fryer to 400°F. Arrange the chicken in a single layer in the greased frying basket. Spray the chicken with cooking oil. Air Fry for 6-7 minutes, then flip the chicken. Cook for another 3 minutes. Serve and enjoy!

Yummy Shredded Chicken

Servings: 2
Cooking Time: 15 Minutes
Ingredients:

- 2 large chicken breasts
- ¼ tsp Pepper
- 1 tsp garlic puree
- 1 tsp mustard
- Salt

Directions:

1. Add all ingredients to the bowl and toss well.
2. Transfer chicken into the air fryer basket and cook at 360°F for 15 minutes.
3. Remove chicken from air fryer and shred using a fork.
4. Serve and enjoy.

Fried Chicken Halves

Servings: 4
Cooking Time: 75 Minutes
Ingredients:

- 16 oz whole chicken
- 1 tablespoon dried thyme
- 1 teaspoon ground cumin
- 1 teaspoon salt
- 1 tablespoon avocado oil

Directions:

1. Cut the chicken into halves and sprinkle it with dried thyme, cumin, and salt. Then brush the chicken halves with avocado oil. Preheat the air fryer to 365°F. Put the chicken halves in the air fryer and cook them for 60 minutes. Then flip the chicken halves on another side and cook them for 15 minutes more.

Buttermilk Brined Turkey Breast

Servings:8
Cooking Time:20 Minutes
Ingredients:

- ¾ cup brine from a can of olives
- 3½ pounds boneless, skinless turkey breast
- 2 fresh thyme sprigs
- 1 fresh rosemary sprig
- ½ cup buttermilk

Directions:

1. Preheat the Air fryer to 350°F and grease an Air fryer basket.
2. Mix olive brine and buttermilk in a bowl until well combined.
3. Place the turkey breast, buttermilk mixture and herb sprigs in a resealable plastic bag.
4. Seal the bag and refrigerate for about 12 hours.
5. Remove the turkey breast from bag and arrange the turkey breast into the Air fryer basket.
6. Cook for about 20 minutes, flipping once in between.
7. Dish out the turkey breast onto a cutting board and cut into desired size slices to serve.

Lemon Pepper Chicken Wings

Servings: 4
Cooking Time: 16 Minutes
Ingredients:

- 1 lb chicken wings
- 1 tsp lemon pepper
- 1 tbsp olive oil
- 1 tsp salt

Directions:

1. Add chicken wings into the large mixing bowl.
2. Add remaining ingredients over chicken and toss well to coat.
3. Place chicken wings in the air fryer basket.
4. Cook chicken wings for 8 minutes at 400°F.
5. Turn chicken wings to another side and cook for 8 minutes more.
6. Serve and enjoy.

Sweet Nutty Chicken Breasts

Servings:4
Cooking Time: 30 Minutes
Ingredients:

- 2 chicken breasts, halved lengthwise
- ¼ cup honey mustard
- ¼ cup chopped pecans
- 1 tbsp olive oil
- 1 tbsp parsley, chopped

Directions:

1. Preheat air fryer to 350°F. Brush chicken breasts with honey mustard and olive oil on all sides. Place the pecans in a bowl. Add and coat the chicken breasts. Place the breasts in the greased frying basket and Air Fry for 25 minutes, turning once. Let chill onto a serving plate for 5 minutes. Sprinkle with parsley and serve.

Gingered Chicken Drumsticks

Servings:3
Cooking Time:25 Minutes
Ingredients:
- ¼ cup full-fat coconut milk
- 3 chicken drumsticks
- 2 teaspoons fresh ginger, minced
- 2 teaspoons galangal, minced
- 2 teaspoons ground turmeric
- Salt, to taste

Directions:
1. Preheat the Air fryer to 375°F and grease an Air fryer basket.
2. Mix the coconut milk, galangal, ginger, and spices in a bowl.
3. Add the chicken drumsticks and coat generously with the marinade.
4. Refrigerate to marinate for at least 8 hours and transfer into the Air fryer basket.
5. Cook for about 25 minutes and dish out the chicken drumsticks onto a serving platter.

Pickle-brined Fried Chicken

Servings:4
Cooking Time: 20 Minutes
Ingredients:
- 4 boneless, skinless chicken thighs
- ⅓ cup dill pickle juice
- 1 large egg
- 2 ounces plain pork rinds, crushed
- ½ teaspoon salt
- ¼ teaspoon ground black pepper

Directions:
1. Place chicken thighs in a large sealable bowl or bag and pour pickle juice over them. Place sealed bowl or bag into refrigerator and allow to marinate at least 1 hour up to overnight.
2. In a small bowl, whisk egg. Place pork rinds in a separate medium bowl.
3. Remove chicken thighs from marinade. Shake off excess pickle juice and pat thighs dry with a paper towel. Sprinkle with salt and pepper.
4. Dip each thigh into egg and gently shake off excess. Press into pork rinds to coat each side. Place thighs into ungreased air fryer basket. Adjust the temperature to 400°F and set the timer for 20 minutes. When chicken thighs are done, they will be golden and crispy on the outside with an internal temperature of at least 165°F. Serve warm.

Chipotle Drumsticks

Servings:4
Cooking Time: 25 Minutes
Ingredients:
- 1 tablespoon tomato paste
- ½ teaspoon chipotle powder
- ¼ teaspoon apple cider vinegar
- ¼ teaspoon garlic powder
- 8 chicken drumsticks
- ½ teaspoon salt
- ⅛ teaspoon ground black pepper

Directions:
1. In a small bowl, combine tomato paste, chipotle powder, vinegar, and garlic powder.
2. Sprinkle drumsticks with salt and pepper, then place into a large bowl and pour in tomato paste mixture. Toss or stir to evenly coat all drumsticks in mixture.
3. Place drumsticks into ungreased air fryer basket. Adjust the temperature to 400°F and set the timer for 25 minutes, turning drumsticks halfway through cooking. Drumsticks will be dark red with an internal temperature of at least 165°F when done. Serve warm.

Crispy Cajun Fried Chicken

Servings: 4
Cooking Time: 50 Minutes
Ingredients:
- 4 boneless, skinless chicken thighs
- ¾ cup buttermilk
- ⅓ cup hot sauce
- 1 ½ tablespoons Cajun seasoning, divided
- 1 cup all-purpose flour
- 1 large egg

Directions:
1. Preheat the air fryer to 375°F.
2. In a large bowl, combine chicken thighs, buttermilk, hot sauce, and ½ tablespoon Cajun seasoning, and toss to coat. Cover and let marinate in refrigerator at least 30 minutes.
3. In a large bowl, whisk flour with ½ tablespoon Cajun seasoning. In a medium bowl, whisk egg.
4. Remove chicken from marinade and sprinkle with remaining ½ tablespoon Cajun seasoning.
5. Dredge chicken by dipping into egg, then pressing into flour to fully coat. Spritz with cooking spray and place into the air fryer basket.
6. Cook 20 minutes, turning halfway through cooking time, until chicken is golden brown and internal temperature reaches at least 165°F. Serve warm.

Ginger Turmeric Chicken Thighs

Servings:4
Cooking Time: 25 Minutes
Ingredients:
- 4 boneless, skin-on chicken thighs
- 2 tablespoons coconut oil, melted
- ½ teaspoon ground turmeric
- ½ teaspoon salt
- ½ teaspoon garlic powder
- ½ teaspoon ground ginger
- ¼ teaspoon ground black pepper

Directions:
1. Place chicken thighs in a large bowl and drizzle with coconut oil. Sprinkle with remaining ingredients and toss to coat both sides of thighs.
2. Place thighs skin side up into ungreased air fryer basket. Adjust the temperature to 400°F and set the timer for 25 minutes. After 10 minutes, turn thighs. When 5 minutes remain, flip thighs once more. Chicken will be done when skin is golden brown and the internal temperature is at least 165°F. Serve warm.

Sticky Drumsticks

Servings: 4
Cooking Time: 45 Minutes
Ingredients:
- 1 lb chicken drumsticks
- 1 tbsp chicken seasoning
- 1 tsp dried chili flakes
- Salt and pepper to taste
- ¼ cup honey
- 1 cup barbecue sauce

Directions:
1. Preheat air fryer to 390°F. Season drumsticks with chicken seasoning, chili flakes, salt, and pepper. Place one batch of drumsticks in the greased frying basket and Air Fry for 18-20 minutes, flipping once until golden.
2. While the chicken is cooking, combine honey and barbecue sauce in a small bowl. Remove the drumsticks to a serving dish. Drizzle honey-barbecue sauce over and serve.

Teriyaki Chicken Kebabs

Servings:4
Cooking Time:1 Hour 15 Minutes
Ingredients:
- ¾ cup teriyaki sauce, divided
- 4 boneless, skinless chicken thighs, cubed
- 1 teaspoon salt
- ½ teaspoon ground black pepper
- 1 cup pineapple chunks
- 1 medium red bell pepper, seeded and cut into 1" cubes
- ¼ medium yellow onion, peeled and cut into 1" cubes

Directions:
1. In a large bowl, pour ½ cup teriyaki sauce over chicken and sprinkle with salt and black pepper. Cover and let marinate in refrigerator 1 hour.
2. Soak eight 6" skewers in water at least 10 minutes to prevent burning. Preheat the air fryer to 400°F.
3. Place a cube of chicken on skewer, then a piece of pineapple, bell pepper, and onion. Repeat with remaining chicken, pineapple, and vegetables.
4. Brush kebabs with remaining ¼ cup teriyaki sauce and place in the air fryer basket. Cook 15 minutes, turning twice during cooking, until chicken reaches an internal temperature of at least 165°F and vegetables are tender. Serve warm.

Cheesy Chicken And Broccoli Casserole

Servings:4
Cooking Time: 30 Minutes
Ingredients:
- 1 pound boneless, skinless chicken breast, cubed
- 1 teaspoon salt
- ½ teaspoon ground black pepper
- 1 cup uncooked instant long-grain white rice
- 1 cup chopped broccoli florets
- 1 cup chicken broth
- 1 cup shredded sharp Cheddar cheese

Directions:
1. Preheat the air fryer to 400°F.
2. In a 6" round baking dish, add chicken and sprinkle with salt and pepper.
3. Place in the air fryer basket and cook 10 minutes, stirring twice during cooking.
4. Add rice, broccoli, broth, and Cheddar. Stir until combined. Cover with foil, being sure to tuck foil under the bottom of the dish to ensure the air fryer fan does not blow it off.
5. Place dish back in the air fryer basket and cook 20 minutes until rice is tender. Serve warm.

Spicy Pork Rind Fried Chicken

Servings:4
Cooking Time: 20 Minutes
Ingredients:

- ¼ cup buffalo sauce
- 4 boneless, skinless chicken breasts
- ½ teaspoon paprika
- ½ teaspoon garlic powder
- ¼ teaspoon ground black pepper
- 2 ounces plain pork rinds, finely crushed

Directions:

1. Pour buffalo sauce into a large sealable bowl or bag. Add chicken and toss to coat. Place sealed bowl or bag into refrigerator and let marinate at least 30 minutes up to overnight.
2. Remove chicken from marinade but do not shake excess sauce off chicken. Sprinkle both sides of thighs with paprika, garlic powder, and pepper.
3. Place pork rinds into a large bowl and press each chicken breast into pork rinds to coat evenly on both sides.
4. Place chicken into ungreased air fryer basket. Adjust the temperature to 400°F and set the timer for 20 minutes, turning chicken halfway through cooking. Chicken will be golden and have an internal temperature of at least 165°F when done. Serve warm.

Bacon-wrapped Chicken

Servings: 6
Cooking Time: 20 Minutes
Ingredients:

- 1 chicken breast, cut into 6 pieces
- 6 rashers back bacon
- 1 tbsp. soft cheese

Directions:

1. Put the bacon rashers on a flat surface and cover one side with the soft cheese.
2. Lay the chicken pieces on each bacon rasher. Wrap the bacon around the chicken and use a toothpick stick to hold each one in place. Put them in Air Fryer basket.
3. Air fry at 350°F for 15 minutes.

Buffalo Chicken Wings

Servings: 3
Cooking Time: 37 Minutes
Ingredients:

- 2 lb. chicken wings
- 1 tsp. salt
- ¼ tsp. black pepper
- 1 cup buffalo sauce

Directions:

1. Wash the chicken wings and pat them dry with clean kitchen towels.
2. Place the chicken wings in a large bowl and sprinkle on salt and pepper.
3. Pre-heat the Air Fryer to 380°F.
4. Place the wings in the fryer and cook for 15 minutes, giving them an occasional stir throughout.
5. Place the wings in a bowl. Pour over the buffalo sauce and toss well to coat.
6. Put the chicken back in the Air Fryer and cook for a final 5 – 6 minutes.

Crispy "fried" Chicken

Servings: 4
Cooking Time: 14 Minutes
Ingredients:

- ¾ cup all-purpose flour
- ½ teaspoon paprika
- ¼ teaspoon black pepper
- ¼ teaspoon salt
- 2 large eggs
- 1½ cups panko breadcrumbs
- 1 pound boneless, skinless chicken tenders

Directions:

1. Preheat the air fryer to 400°F.
2. In a shallow bowl, mix the flour with the paprika, pepper, and salt.
3. In a separate bowl, whisk the eggs; set aside.
4. In a third bowl, place the breadcrumbs.
5. Liberally spray the air fryer basket with olive oil spray.
6. Pat the chicken tenders dry with a paper towel. Dredge the tenders one at a time in the flour, then dip them in the egg, and toss them in the breadcrumb coating. Repeat until all tenders are coated.
7. Set each tender in the air fryer, leaving room on each side of the tender to allow for flipping.
8. When the basket is full, cook 4 to 7 minutes, flip, and cook another 4 to 7 minutes.
9. Remove the tenders and let cool 5 minutes before serving. Repeat until all tenders are cooked.

Chicken Wrapped In Bacon

Servings: 6
Cooking Time: 25 Minutes
Ingredients:
- 6 rashers unsmoked back bacon
- 1 small chicken breast
- 1 tbsp. garlic soft cheese

Directions:
1. Cut the chicken breast into six bite-sized pieces.
2. Spread the soft cheese across one side of each slice of bacon.
3. Put the chicken on top of the cheese and wrap the bacon around it, holding it in place with a toothpick.
4. Transfer the wrapped chicken pieces to the Air Fryer and cook for 15 minutes at 350°F.

Butter And Bacon Chicken

Servings:6
Cooking Time: 65 Minutes
Ingredients:
- 1 whole chicken
- 2 tablespoons salted butter, softened
- 1 teaspoon dried thyme
- ½ teaspoon garlic powder
- 1 teaspoon salt
- ½ teaspoon ground black pepper
- 6 slices sugar-free bacon

Directions:
1. Pat chicken dry with a paper towel, then rub with butter on all sides. Sprinkle thyme, garlic powder, salt, and pepper over chicken.
2. Place chicken into ungreased air fryer basket, breast side up. Lay strips of bacon over chicken and secure with toothpicks.
3. Adjust the temperature to 350°F and set the timer for 65 minutes. Halfway through cooking, remove and set aside bacon and flip chicken over. Chicken will be done when the skin is golden and crispy and the internal temperature is at least 165°F. Serve warm with bacon.

Stuffed Chicken

Servings: 2
Cooking Time: 11 Minutes
Ingredients:
- 8 oz chicken fillet
- 3 oz Blue cheese
- ½ teaspoon salt
- ½ teaspoon thyme
- 1 teaspoon sesame oil

Directions:
1. Cut the fillet into halves and beat them gently with the help of the kitchen hammer. After this, make the horizontal cut in every fillet. Sprinkle the chicken with salt and thyme. Then fill it with Blue cheese and secure the cut with the help of the toothpick. Sprinkle the stuffed chicken fillets with sesame oil. Preheat the air fryer to 385°F. Put the chicken fillets in the air fryer and cook them for 7 minutes. Then carefully flip the chicken fillets on another side and cook for 4 minutes more.

Chicken Pesto Pizzas

Servings:4
Cooking Time: 12 Minutes
Ingredients:
- 1 pound ground chicken thighs
- ¼ teaspoon salt
- ⅛ teaspoon ground black pepper
- ¼ cup basil pesto
- 1 cup shredded mozzarella cheese
- 4 grape tomatoes, sliced

Directions:
1. Cut four squares of parchment paper to fit into your air fryer basket.
2. Place ground chicken in a large bowl and mix with salt and pepper. Divide mixture into four equal sections.
3. Wet your hands with water to prevent sticking, then press each section into a 6" circle onto a piece of ungreased parchment. Place each chicken crust into air fryer basket, working in batches if needed.
4. Adjust the temperature to 350°F and set the timer for 10 minutes, turning crusts halfway through cooking.
5. When the timer beeps, spread 1 tablespoon pesto across the top of each crust, then sprinkle with ¼ cup mozzarella and top with 1 sliced tomato. Continue cooking at 350°F for 2 minutes. Cheese will be melted and brown when done. Serve warm.

Grilled Chicken Pesto

Servings:8
Cooking Time: 30 Minutes
Ingredients:
- 1 ¾ cup commercial pesto
- 8 chicken thighs
- Salt and pepper to taste

Directions:
1. Place all Ingredients in the Ziploc bag and allow to marinate in the fridge for at least 2 hours.
2. Preheat the air fryer to 390°F.
3. Place the grill pan accessory in the air fryer.
4. Grill the chicken for at least 30 minutes.
5. Make sure to flip the chicken every 10 minutes for even grilling.

Peppery Lemon-chicken Breast

Servings:1
Cooking Time:
Ingredients:
- 1 chicken breast
- 1 teaspoon minced garlic
- 2 lemons, rinds and juice reserved
- Salt and pepper to taste

Directions:
1. Preheat the air fryer.
2. Place all ingredients in a baking dish that will fit in the air fryer.
3. Place in the air fryer basket.
4. Close and cook for 20 minutes at 400°F.

Baked Chicken Nachos

Servings:4
Cooking Time: 7 Minutes
Ingredients:
- 50 tortilla chips
- 2 cups shredded cooked chicken breast, divided
- 2 cups shredded Mexican-blend cheese, divided
- ½ cup sliced pickled jalapeño peppers, divided
- ½ cup diced red onion, divided

Directions:
1. Preheat the air fryer to 300°F.
2. Use foil to make a bowl shape that fits the shape of the air fryer basket. Place half tortilla chips in the bottom of foil bowl, then top with 1 cup chicken, 1 cup cheese, ¼ cup jalapeños, and ¼ cup onion. Repeat with remaining chips and toppings.

3. Place foil bowl in the air fryer basket and cook 7 minutes until cheese is melted and toppings heated through. Serve warm.

Balsamic Duck And Cranberry Sauce

Servings: 4
Cooking Time: 25 Minutes
Ingredients:
- 4 duck breasts, boneless, skin-on and scored
- A pinch of salt and black pepper
- 1 tablespoon olive oil
- ¼ cup balsamic vinegar
- ½ cup dried cranberries

Directions:
1. Heat up a pan that fits your air fryer with the oil over medium-high heat, add the duck breasts skin side down and cook for 5 minutes. Add the rest of the ingredients, toss, put the pan in the fryer and cook at 380°F for 20 minutes. Divide between plates and serve.

Garlic Dill Wings

Servings:4
Cooking Time: 25 Minutes
Ingredients:
- 2 pounds bone-in chicken wings, separated at joints
- ½ teaspoon salt
- ½ teaspoon ground black pepper
- ½ teaspoon onion powder
- ½ teaspoon garlic powder
- 1 teaspoon dried dill

Directions:
1. In a large bowl, toss wings with salt, pepper, onion powder, garlic powder, and dill until evenly coated. Place wings into ungreased air fryer basket in a single layer, working in batches if needed.
2. Adjust the temperature to 400°F and set the timer for 25 minutes, shaking the basket every 7 minutes during cooking. Wings should have an internal temperature of at least 165°F and be golden brown when done. Serve warm.

Air Fried Cheese Chicken

Servings:6
Cooking Time: 15 Minutes
Ingredients:
- 6 tbsp seasoned breadcrumbs
- 2 tbsp Parmesan cheese, grated
- 1 tbsp melted butter
- ½ cup mozzarella cheese, shredded
- 1 tbsp marinara sauce
- Cooking spray as needed

Directions:
1. Preheat your air fryer to 390°F. Grease the cooking basket with cooking spray. In a small bowl, mix breadcrumbs and Parmesan cheese. Brush the chicken pieces with butter and dredge into the breadcrumbs. Add chicken to the cooking basket and cook for 6 minutes. Turn over and top with marinara sauce and shredded mozzarella; cook for 3 more minutes.

Air Fried Chicken Tenderloin

Servings:8
Cooking Time: 15 Minutes
Ingredients:
- ½ cup almond flour
- 1 egg, beaten
- 2 tablespoons coconut oil
- 8 chicken tenderloins
- Salt and pepper to taste

Directions:
1. Preheat the air fryer for 5 minutes.
2. Season the chicken tenderloin with salt and pepper to taste.
3. Soak in beaten eggs then dredge in almond flour.
4. Place in the air fryer and brush with coconut oil.
5. Cook for 15 minutes at 375°F.
6. Halfway through the cooking time, give the fryer basket a shake to cook evenly.

Italian Chicken Thighs

Servings: 4
Cooking Time: 30 Minutes
Ingredients:
- 4 skin-on bone-in chicken thighs
- 2 tbsp. unsalted butter, melted
- 3 tsp. Italian herbs
- ½ tsp. garlic powder
- ¼ tsp. onion powder

Directions:
1. Using a brush, coat the chicken thighs with the melted butter. Combine the herbs with the garlic powder and onion powder, then massage into the chicken thighs. Place the thighs in the fryer.
2. Cook at 380°F for 20 minutes, turning the chicken halfway through to cook on the other side.
3. When the thighs have achieved a golden color, test the temperature with a meat thermometer. Once they have reached 165°F, remove from the fryer and serve.

Chicken Parmesan Casserole

Servings:4
Cooking Time: 20 Minutes
Ingredients:
- 2 cups cubed cooked chicken breast
- ½ teaspoon salt
- ¼ teaspoon ground black pepper
- ¾ cup marinara sauce
- 2 teaspoons Italian seasoning, divided
- 1 cup shredded mozzarella cheese
- ½ cup grated Parmesan cheese

Directions:
1. Preheat the air fryer to 320°F.
2. In a large bowl, toss chicken with salt, pepper, marinara, and 1 teaspoon Italian seasoning.
3. Scrape mixture into a 6" round baking dish. Top with mozzarella, Parmesan, and remaining 1 teaspoon Italian seasoning.
4. Place in the air fryer basket and cook 20 minutes until the sauce is bubbling and cheese is brown and melted. Serve warm.

Tangy Mustard Wings

Servings:4
Cooking Time: 25 Minutes
Ingredients:
- 1 pound bone-in chicken wings, separated at joints
- ¼ cup yellow mustard
- ½ teaspoon salt
- ¼ teaspoon ground black pepper

Directions:
1. Place wings in a large bowl and toss with mustard to fully coat. Sprinkle with salt and pepper.
2. Place wings into ungreased air fryer basket. Adjust the temperature to 400°F and set the timer for 25 minutes, shaking the basket three times during cooking. Wings will be done when browned and cooked to an internal temperature of at least 165°F. Serve warm.

Zesty Ranch Chicken Drumsticks

Servings: 4
Cooking Time: 20 Minutes
Ingredients:
- 8 chicken drumsticks
- 1 teaspoon salt
- ½ teaspoon ground black pepper
- ¼ cup dry ranch seasoning
- ½ cup panko bread crumbs
- ½ cup grated Parmesan cheese

Directions:
1. Preheat the air fryer to 375°F.
2. Sprinkle drumsticks with salt, pepper, and ranch seasoning.
3. In a paper lunch bag, combine bread crumbs and Parmesan. Add drumsticks to the bag and shake to coat. Spritz with cooking spray.
4. Place drumsticks in the air fryer basket and cook 20 minutes, turning halfway through cooking time, until the internal temperature reaches at least 165°F. Serve warm.

Blackened Chicken Tenders

Servings:4
Cooking Time: 12 Minutes
Ingredients:
- 1 pound boneless, skinless chicken tenders
- 2 teaspoons paprika
- 1 teaspoon garlic powder
- 1 teaspoon salt
- ½ teaspoon cayenne pepper
- ½ teaspoon dried thyme
- ½ teaspoon ground black pepper
- Cooking spray

Directions:
1. Preheat the air fryer to 400°F.
2. Place chicken tenders into a large bowl.
3. In a small bowl, mix paprika, garlic powder, salt, cayenne, thyme, and black pepper. Add spice mixture to chicken and toss to coat. Spritz chicken with cooking spray.
4. Place chicken in the air fryer basket and cook 12 minutes, turning halfway through cooking time, until chicken is brown at the edges and internal temperature reaches at least 165°F. Serve warm.

Teriyaki Chicken Legs

Servings: 2
Cooking Time: 20 Minutes
Ingredients:
- 4 tablespoons teriyaki sauce
- 1 tablespoon orange juice
- 1 teaspoon smoked paprika
- 4 chicken legs
- cooking spray

Directions:
1. Mix together the teriyaki sauce, orange juice, and smoked paprika. Brush on all sides of chicken legs.
2. Spray air fryer basket with nonstick cooking spray and place chicken in basket.
3. Cook at 360°F for 6minutes. Turn and baste with sauce. Cook for 6 moreminutes, turn and baste. Cook for 8 minutes more, until juices run clear when chicken is pierced with a fork.

Simple Salsa Chicken Thighs

Servings:2
Cooking Time: 35 Minutes
Ingredients:
- 1 lb boneless, skinless chicken thighs
- 1 cup mild chunky salsa
- ½ tsp taco seasoning
- 2 lime wedges for serving

Directions:
1. Preheat air fryer to 350°F. Add chicken thighs into a baking pan and pour salsa and taco seasoning over. Place the pan in the frying basket and Air Fry for 30 minutes until golden brown. Serve with lime wedges.

Chipotle Aioli Wings

Servings:6
Cooking Time: 25 Minutes
Ingredients:
- 2 pounds bone-in chicken wings
- ½ teaspoon salt
- ¼ teaspoon ground black pepper
- 2 tablespoons mayonnaise
- 2 teaspoons chipotle powder
- 2 tablespoons lemon juice

Directions:
1. In a large bowl, toss wings in salt and pepper, then place into ungreased air fryer basket. Adjust the temperature to 400°F and set the timer for 25 minutes, shaking the basket twice while cooking. Wings will be done when golden and have an internal temperature of at least 165°F.
2. In a small bowl, whisk together mayonnaise, chipotle powder, and lemon juice. Place cooked wings into a large serving bowl and drizzle with aioli. Toss to coat. Serve warm.

Basic Chicken Breasts.

Servings:4
Cooking Time: 15 Minutes
Ingredients:

- 2 tsp olive oil
- 2 chicken breasts
- Salt and pepper to taste
- ½ tsp garlic powder
- ½ tsp rosemary

Directions:

1. Preheat air fryer to 350°F. Rub the chicken breasts with olive oil over tops and bottom and sprinkle with garlic powder, rosemary, salt, and pepper. Place the chicken in the frying basket and Air Fry for 9 minutes, flipping once. Let rest onto a serving plate for 5 minutes before cutting into cubes. Serve and enjoy!

Pretzel-crusted Chicken

Servings:4
Cooking Time: 12 Minutes
Ingredients:

- 2 cups mini twist pretzels
- ½ cup mayonnaise
- 2 tablespoons honey
- 2 tablespoons yellow mustard
- 4 boneless, skinless chicken breasts, sliced in half lengthwise
- 1 teaspoon salt
- ½ teaspoon ground black pepper
- Cooking spray

Directions:

1. Preheat the air fryer to 375°F.
2. In a food processor, place pretzels and pulse ten times.
3. In a medium bowl, mix mayonnaise, honey, and mustard.
4. Sprinkle chicken with salt and pepper, then brush with sauce mixture until well coated.
5. Pour pretzel crumbs onto a shallow plate and press each piece of chicken into them until well coated.
6. Spritz chicken with cooking spray and place in the air fryer basket. Cook 12 minutes, turning halfway through cooking time, until edges are golden brown and the internal temperature reaches at least 165°F. Serve warm.

Herb Seasoned Turkey Breast

Servings: 4
Cooking Time: 35 Minutes

Ingredients:

- 2 lbs turkey breast
- 1 tsp fresh sage, chopped
- 1 tsp fresh rosemary, chopped
- 1 tsp fresh thyme, chopped
- Pepper
- Salt

Directions:

1. Spray air fryer basket with cooking spray.
2. In a small bowl, mix together sage, rosemary, and thyme.
3. Season turkey breast with pepper and salt and rub with herb mixture.
4. Place turkey breast in air fryer basket and cook at 390°F for 30-35 minutes.
5. Slice and serve.

Buttermilk-fried Drumsticks

Servings: 2
Cooking Time: 25 Minutes
Ingredients:

- 1 egg
- ½ cup buttermilk
- ¾ cup self-rising flour
- ¾ cup seasoned panko breadcrumbs
- 1 teaspoon salt
- ¼ teaspoon ground black pepper (to mix into coating)
- 4 chicken drumsticks, skin on
- oil for misting or cooking spray

Directions:

1. Beat together egg and buttermilk in shallow dish.
2. In a second shallow dish, combine the flour, panko crumbs, salt, and pepper.
3. Sprinkle chicken legs with additional salt and pepper to taste.
4. Dip legs in buttermilk mixture, then roll in panko mixture, pressing in crumbs to make coating stick. Mist with oil or cooking spray.
5. Spray air fryer basket with cooking spray.
6. Cook drumsticks at 360°F for 10 minutes. Turn pieces over and cook an additional 10minutes.
7. Turn pieces to check for browning. If you have any white spots that haven't begun to brown, spritz them with oil or cooking spray. Continue cooking for 5 more minutes or until crust is golden brown and juices run clear. Larger, meatier drumsticks will take longer to cook than small ones.

Chicken Thighs In Salsa Verde

Servings: 4
Cooking Time: 35 Minutes
Ingredients:

- 4 boneless, skinless chicken thighs
- 1 cup salsa verde
- 1 tsp mashed garlic

Directions:

1. Preheat air fryer at 350°F. Add chicken thighs to a cake pan and cover with salsa verde and mashed garlic. Place cake pan in the frying basket and Bake for 30 minutes. Let rest for 5 minutes before serving.

Creamy Onion Chicken

Servings:4
Cooking Time: 20 Minutes
Ingredients:

- 1 ½ cup onion soup mix
- 1 cup mushroom soup
- ½ cup cream

Directions:

1. Preheat Fryer to 400°F. Add mushrooms, onion mix and cream in a frying pan. Heat on low heat for 1 minute. Pour the warm mixture over chicken slices and allow to sit for 25 minutes. Place the marinated chicken in the air fryer cooking basket and cook for 15 minutes. Serve with the remaining cream.

Bacon Chicken Mix

Servings: 2
Cooking Time: 25 Minutes
Ingredients:

- 2 chicken legs
- 4 oz bacon, sliced
- ½ teaspoon salt
- ½ teaspoon ground black pepper
- 1 teaspoon sesame oil

Directions:

1. Sprinkle the chicken legs with salt and ground black pepper and wrap in the sliced bacon. After this, preheat the air fryer to 385°F. Put the chicken legs in the air fryer and sprinkle with sesame oil. Cook the bacon chicken legs for 25 minutes.

Spinach And Feta Stuffed Chicken Breasts

Servings: 4
Cooking Time: 27 Minutes
Ingredients:

- 1 package frozen spinach, thawed and drained well
- 1 cup feta cheese, crumbled
- ½ teaspoon freshly ground black pepper
- 4 boneless chicken breasts
- salt and freshly ground black pepper
- 1 tablespoon olive oil

Directions:

1. Prepare the filling. Squeeze out as much liquid as possible from the thawed spinach. Rough chop the spinach and transfer it to a mixing bowl with the feta cheese and the freshly ground black pepper.

2. Prepare the chicken breast. Place the chicken breast on a cutting board and press down on the chicken breast with one hand to keep it stabilized. Make an incision about 1-inch long in the fattest side of the breast. Move the knife up and down inside the chicken breast, without poking through either the top or the bottom, or the other side of the breast. The inside pocket should be about 3-inches long, but the opening should only be about 1-inch wide. If this is too difficult, you can make the incision longer, but you will have to be more careful when cooking the chicken breast since this will expose more of the stuffing.

3. Once you have prepared the chicken breasts, use your fingers to stuff the filling into each pocket, spreading the mixture down as far as you can.

4. Preheat the air fryer to 380°F.

5. Lightly brush or spray the air fryer basket and the chicken breasts with olive oil. Transfer two of the stuffed chicken breasts to the air fryer. Air-fry for 12 minutes, turning the chicken breasts over halfway through the cooking time. Remove the chicken to a resting plate and air-fry the second two breasts for 12 minutes. Return the first batch of chicken to the air fryer with the second batch and air-fry for 3 more minutes. When the chicken is cooked, an instant read thermometer should register 165°F in the thickest part of the chicken, as well as in the stuffing.

6. Remove the chicken breasts and let them rest on a cutting board for 2 to 3 minutes. Slice the chicken on the bias and serve with the slices fanned out.

Chicken Chunks

Servings: 4
Cooking Time: 10 Minutes
Ingredients:
- 1 pound chicken tenders cut in large chunks, about 1½ inches
- salt and pepper
- ½ cup cornstarch
- 2 eggs, beaten
- 1 cup panko breadcrumbs
- oil for misting or cooking spray

Directions:
1. Season chicken chunks to your liking with salt and pepper.
2. Dip chicken chunks in cornstarch. Then dip in egg and shake off excess. Then roll in panko crumbs to coat well.
3. Spray all sides of chicken chunks with oil or cooking spray.
4. Place chicken in air fryer basket in single layer and cook at 390°F for 5minutes. Spray with oil, turn chunks over, and spray other side.
5. Cook for an additional 5minutes or until chicken juices run clear and outside is golden brown.
6. Repeat steps 4 and 5 to cook remaining chicken.

Harissa Chicken Wings

Servings: 4
Cooking Time: 25 Minutes
Ingredients:
- 8 whole chicken wings
- 1 tsp garlic powder
- ¼ tsp dried oregano
- 1 tbsp harissa seasoning

Directions:
1. Preheat air fryer to 400°F. Season the wings with garlic, harissa seasoning, and oregano. Place them in the greased frying basket and spray with cooking oil spray. Air Fry for 10 minutes, shake the basket, and cook for another 5-7 minutes until golden and crispy. Serve warm.

Mustardy Chicken Bites

Servings: 4
Cooking Time: 20 Minutes + Chilling Time
Ingredients:
- 2 tbsp horseradish mustard
- 1 tbsp mayonnaise
- 1 tbsp olive oil
- 2 chicken breasts, cubes
- 1 tbsp parsley

Directions:
1. Combine all ingredients, excluding parsley, in a bowl. Let marinate covered in the fridge for 30 minutes. Preheat air fryer at 350°F. Place chicken cubes in the greased frying basket and Air Fry for 9 minutes, tossing once. Serve immediately sprinkled with parsley.

Fried Herbed Chicken Wings

Servings: 4
Cooking Time: 11 Minutes
Ingredients:
- 1 tablespoon Emperor herbs chicken spices
- 8 chicken wings
- Cooking spray

Directions:
1. Generously sprinkle the chicken wings with Emperor herbs chicken spices and place in the preheated to 400°F air fryer. Cook the chicken wings for 6 minutes from each side.

Desserts And Sweets Recipes

Easy Keto Danish

Servings:6
Cooking Time: 12 Minutes
Ingredients:
- 1½ cups shredded mozzarella cheese
- ½ cup blanched finely ground almond flour
- 3 ounces cream cheese, divided
- ¼ cup confectioners' erythritol
- 1 tablespoon lemon juice

Directions:
1. Place mozzarella, flour, and 1 ounce cream cheese in a large microwave-safe bowl. Microwave on high 45 seconds, then stir with a fork until a soft dough forms.
2. Separate dough into six equal sections and press each in a single layer into an ungreased 4" × 4" square nonstick baking dish to form six even squares that touch.
3. In a small bowl, mix remaining cream cheese, erythritol, and lemon juice. Place 1 tablespoon mixture in center of each piece of dough in baking dish. Fold all four corners of each dough piece halfway to center to reach cream cheese mixture.
4. Place dish into air fryer. Adjust the temperature to 320°F and set the timer for 12 minutes. The center and edges will be browned when done. Let cool 10 minutes before serving.

Cinnamon-sugar Pretzel Bites

Servings:4
Cooking Time: 1 Hour 10 Minutes
Ingredients:
- 1 cup all-purpose flour
- 1 teaspoon quick-rise yeast
- 2 tablespoons granulated sugar, divided
- ¼ teaspoon salt
- 1 tablespoon olive oil
- ⅓ cup warm water
- 2 teaspoons baking soda
- 1 teaspoon ground cinnamon
- Cooking spray

Directions:
1. In a large bowl, mix flour, yeast, 2 teaspoons sugar, and salt until combined.
2. Pour in oil and water and stir until a dough begins to form and pull away from the edges of the bowl. Remove dough from the bowl and transfer to a lightly floured surface. Knead 10 minutes until dough is mostly smooth.
3. Spritz dough with cooking spray and place into a large clean bowl. Cover with plastic wrap and let rise 1 hour.
4. Preheat the air fryer to 400°F.
5. Press dough into a 6" × 4" rectangle. Cut dough into twenty-four even pieces.
6. Fill a medium saucepan over medium-high heat halfway with water and bring to a boil. Add baking soda and let it boil 1 minute, then add pretzel bites. You may need to work in batches. Cook 45 seconds, then remove from water and drain. They will be puffy but should have mostly maintained their shape.
7. Spritz pretzel bites with cooking spray. Place in the air fryer basket and cook 5 minutes until golden brown.
8. In a small bowl, mix remaining sugar and cinnamon. When pretzel bites are done cooking, immediately toss in cinnamon and sugar mixture and serve.

Nutella And Banana Pastries

Servings:4
Cooking Time:12 Minutes
Ingredients:
- 1 puff pastry sheet, cut into 4 equal squares
- ½ cup Nutella
- 2 bananas, sliced
- 2 tablespoons icing sugar

Directions:
1. Preheat the Air fryer to 375°F and grease an Air fryer basket.
2. Spread Nutella on each pastry square and top with banana slices and icing sugar.
3. Fold each square into a triangle and slightly press the edges with a fork.
4. Arrange the pastries in the Air fryer basket and cook for about 12 minutes.
5. Dish out and serve immediately.

Olive Oil Cake

Servings:8
Cooking Time: 30 Minutes
Ingredients:

- 2 cups blanched finely ground almond flour
- 5 large eggs, whisked
- ¾ cup extra-virgin olive oil
- ⅓ cup granular erythritol
- 1 teaspoon vanilla extract
- 1 teaspoon baking powder

Directions:

1. In a large bowl, mix all ingredients. Pour batter into an ungreased 6" round nonstick baking dish.
2. Place dish into air fryer basket. Adjust the temperature to 300°F and set the timer for 30 minutes. The cake will be golden on top and firm in the center when done.
3. Let cake cool in dish 30 minutes before slicing and serving.

Fried Snickers Bars

Servings:8
Cooking Time: 4 Minutes
Ingredients:

- ⅓ cup All-purpose flour
- 1 Large egg white(s), beaten until foamy
- 1½ cups Vanilla wafer cookie crumbs
- 8 Fun-size Snickers bars, frozen
- Vegetable oil spray

Directions:

1. Preheat the air fryer to 400°F.
2. Set up and fill three shallow soup plates or small pie plates on your counter: one for the flour, one for the beaten egg white(s), and one for the cookie crumbs.
3. Unwrap the frozen candy bars. Dip one in the flour, turning it to coat on all sides. Gently shake off any excess, then set it in the beaten egg white(s). Turn it to coat all sides, even the ends, then let any excess egg white slip back into the rest. Set the candy bar in the cookie crumbs. Turn to coat on all sides, even the ends. Dip the candy bar back in the egg white(s) a second time, then into the cookie crumbs a second time, making sure you have an even coating all around. Coat the covered candy bar all over with vegetable oil spray. Set aside so you can dip and coat the remaining candy bars.
4. Set the coated candy bars in the basket with as much air space between them as possible. Air-fry undisturbed for 4 minutes, or until golden brown.

5. Remove the basket from the machine and let the candy bars cool in the basket for 10 minutes. Use a nonstick-safe spatula to transfer them to a wire rack and cool for 5 minutes more before chowing down.

Apple Dumplings

Servings: 4
Cooking Time: 10 Minutes
Ingredients:

- 4 Small tart apples, preferably McIntosh, peeled and cored
- ¼ cup Granulated white sugar
- 1½ tablespoons Ground cinnamon
- 1 sheet, thawed and cut into four quarters A 17.25-ounce box frozen puff pastry (vegetarian, if a concern)

Directions:

1. Set the apples stem side up on a microwave-safe plate, preferably a glass pie plate. Microwave on high for 3 minutes, or until somewhat tender when poked with the point of a knife. Cool to room temperature, about 30 minutes.
2. Preheat the air fryer to 400°F.
3. Combine the sugar and cinnamon in a small bowl. Roll the apples in this mixture, coating them completely on their outsides. Also sprinkle this cinnamon sugar into each hole where the core was.
4. Roll the puff pastry squares into 6 x 6-inch squares. Slice the corners off each rolled square so that it's sort of like a circle. Place an apple in the center of one of these squares and fold it up and all around the apple, sealing it at the top by pressing the pastry together. The apple must be completely sealed in the pastry. Repeat for the remaining apples.
5. Set the pastry-covered apples in the basket with at least ½ inch between them. Air-fry undisturbed for 10 minutes, or until puffed and golden brown.
6. Use a nonstick-safe spatula, and maybe a flatware tablespoon for balance, to transfer the apples to a wire rack. Cool for at least 5 minutes or up to 15 minutes before serving warm.

Hearty Banana Pastry

Servings:2
Cooking Time: 15 Minutes
Ingredients:

- 3 tbsp honey
- 2 puff pastry sheets, cut into thin strips
- fresh berries to serve

Directions:

1. Preheat your air fryer up to 340°F.
2. Place the banana slices into the cooking basket. Cover with the pastry strips and top with honey. Cook for 10 minutes. Serve with fresh berries.

Pumpkin Pie–spiced Pork Rinds

Servings:4

Cooking Time: 5 Minutes

Ingredients:

- 3 ounces plain pork rinds
- 2 tablespoons salted butter, melted
- 1 teaspoon pumpkin pie spice
- ¼ cup confectioners' erythritol

Directions:

1. In a large bowl, toss pork rinds in butter. Sprinkle with pumpkin pie spice, then toss to evenly coat.
2. Place pork rinds into ungreased air fryer basket. Adjust the temperature to 400°F and set the timer for 5 minutes. Pork rinds will be golden when done.
3. Transfer rinds to a medium serving bowl and sprinkle with erythritol. Serve immediately.

Pecan Snowball Cookies

Servings:12

Cooking Time: 24 Minutes

Ingredients:

- 1 cup chopped pecans
- ½ cup salted butter, melted
- ½ cup coconut flour
- ¾ cup confectioners' erythritol, divided
- 1 teaspoon vanilla extract

Directions:

1. In a food processor, blend together pecans, butter, flour, ½ cup erythritol, and vanilla 1 minute until a dough forms.
2. Form dough into twelve individual cookie balls, about 1 tablespoon each.
3. Cut three pieces of parchment to fit air fryer basket. Place four cookies on each ungreased parchment and place one piece parchment with cookies into air fryer basket. Adjust air fryer temperature to 325°F and set the timer for 8 minutes. Repeat cooking with remaining batches.
4. When the timer goes off, allow cookies to cool 5 minutes on a large serving plate until cool enough to handle. While still warm, dust cookies with remaining erythritol. Allow to cool completely, about 15 minutes, before serving.

Easy Churros

Servings: 12

Cooking Time: 10 Minutes

Ingredients:

- ½ cup Water
- 4 tablespoons (¼ cup/½ stick) Butter
- ¼ teaspoon Table salt
- ½ cup All-purpose flour
- 2 Large egg(s)
- ¼ cup Granulated white sugar
- 2 teaspoons Ground cinnamon

Directions:

1. Bring the water, butter, and salt to a boil in a small saucepan set over high heat, stirring occasionally.
2. When the butter has fully melted, reduce the heat to medium and stir in the flour to form a dough. Continue cooking, stirring constantly, to dry out the dough until it coats the bottom and sides of the pan with a film, even a crust. Remove the pan from the heat, scrape the dough into a bowl, and cool for 15 minutes.
3. Using an electric hand mixer at medium speed, beat in the egg, or eggs one at a time, until the dough is smooth and firm enough to hold its shape.
4. Mix the sugar and cinnamon in a small bowl. Scoop up 1 tablespoon of the dough and roll it in the sugar mixture to form a small, coated tube about ½ inch in diameter and 2 inches long. Set it aside and make 5 more tubes for the small batch or 11 more for the large one.
5. Set the tubes on a plate and freeze for 20 minutes. Meanwhile, Preheat the air fryer to 375°F .
6. Set 3 frozen tubes in the basket for a small batch or 6 for a large one with as much air space between them as possible. Air-fry undisturbed for 10 minutes, or until puffed, brown, and set.
7. Use kitchen tongs to transfer the churros to a wire rack to cool for at least 5 minutes. Meanwhile, air-fry and cool the second batch of churros in the same way.

Chilled Strawberry Pie

Servings:6

Cooking Time: 10 Minutes

Ingredients:

- 1½ cups whole shelled pecans
- 1 tablespoon unsalted butter, softened
- 1 cup heavy whipping cream
- 12 medium fresh strawberries, hulled
- 2 tablespoons sour cream

Directions:

1. Place pecans and butter into a food processor and pulse ten times until a dough forms. Press dough into the bottom of an ungreased 6" round nonstick baking dish.

2. Place dish into air fryer basket. Adjust the temperature to 320°F and set the timer for 10 minutes. Crust will be firm and golden when done. Let cool 20 minutes.

3. In a large bowl, whisk cream until fluffy and doubled in size, about 2 minutes.

4. In a separate large bowl, mash strawberries until mostly liquid. Fold strawberries and sour cream into whipped cream.

5. Spoon mixture into cooled crust, cover, and place into refrigerator for at least 30 minutes to set. Serve chilled.

Cinnamon Canned Biscuit Donuts

Servings: 4
Cooking Time: 25 Minutes
Ingredients:
- 1 can jumbo biscuits
- 1 cup cinnamon sugar

Directions:
1. Preheat air fryer to 360°F. Divide biscuit dough into 8 biscuits and place on a flat work surface. Cut a small circle in the center of the biscuit with a small cookie cutter. Place a batch of 4 donuts in the air fryer. Spray with oil and Bake for 8 minutes, flipping once. Drizzle the cinnamon sugar over the donuts and serve.

Cocoa Bombs

Servings: 12
Cooking Time: 8 Minutes
Ingredients:
- 2 cups macadamia nuts, chopped
- 4 tablespoons coconut oil, melted
- 1 teaspoon vanilla extract
- ¼ cup cocoa powder
- 1/3 cup swerve

Directions:
1. In a bowl, mix all the ingredients and whisk well. Shape medium balls out of this mix, place them in your air fryer and cook at 300°F for 8 minutes. Serve cold.

Keto Butter Balls

Servings: 4
Cooking Time: 10 Minutes
Ingredients:
- 1 tablespoon butter, softened1 tablespoon Erythritol
- ½ teaspoon ground cinnamon
- 1 tablespoon coconut flour

- 1 teaspoon coconut flakes
- Cooking spray

Directions:
1. Put the butter, Erythritol, ground cinnamon, coconut flour, and coconut flakes. Then stir the mixture with the help of the fork until homogenous. Make 4 balls. Preheat the air fryer to 375°F. Spray the air fryer basket with cooking spray and place the balls inside. Cook the dessert for 10 minutes.

Party S´mores

Servings: 6
Cooking Time: 15 Minutes
Ingredients:
- 2 dark chocolate bars, cut into 12 pieces
- 12 buttermilk biscuits
- 12 marshmallows

Directions:
1. Preheat air fryer to 350°F. Place 6 biscuits in the air fryer. Top each square with a piece of dark chocolate. Bake for 2 minutes. Add a marshmallow to each piece of chocolate. Cook for another minute. Remove and top with another piece of biscuit. Serve warm.

Grape Stew

Servings: 4
Cooking Time: 14 Minutes
Ingredients:
- 1 pound red grapes
- Juice and zest of 1 lemon
- 26 ounces grape juice

Directions:
1. In a pan that fits your air fryer, add all ingredients and toss.

2. Place the pan in the fryer and cook at 320°F for 14 minutes.

3. Divide into cups, refrigerate, and serve cold.

Fried Oreos

Servings: 12
Cooking Time: 6 Minutes Per Batch
Ingredients:
- oil for misting or nonstick spray
- 1 cup complete pancake and waffle mix
- 1 teaspoon vanilla extract
- ½ cup water, plus 2 tablespoons
- 12 Oreos or other chocolate sandwich cookies
- 1 tablespoon confectioners' sugar

Directions:
1. Spray baking pan with oil or nonstick spray and place in basket.
2. Preheat air fryer to 390°F.
3. In a medium bowl, mix together the pancake mix, vanilla, and water.
4. Dip 4 cookies in batter and place in baking pan.
5. Cook for 6minutes, until browned.
6. Repeat steps 4 and 5 for the remaining cookies.
7. Sift sugar over warm cookies.

Brown Sugar Cookies

Servings:9
Cooking Time: 27 Minutes
Ingredients:
- 4 tablespoons salted butter, melted
- ⅓ cup granular brown erythritol
- 1 large egg
- ½ teaspoon vanilla extract
- 1 cup blanched finely ground almond flour
- ½ teaspoon baking powder

Directions:
1. In a large bowl, whisk together butter, erythritol, egg, and vanilla. Add flour and baking powder, and stir until combined.
2. Separate dough into nine pieces and roll into balls, about 2 tablespoons each.
3. Cut three pieces of parchment paper to fit your air fryer basket and place three cookies on each ungreased piece. Place one piece of parchment into air fryer basket. Adjust the temperature to 300°F and set the timer for 9 minutes. Edges of cookies will be browned when done. Repeat with remaining cookies. Serve warm.

Coconut Flour Cake

Servings:6
Cooking Time: 25 Minutes
Ingredients:
- 2 tablespoons salted butter, melted
- ⅓ cup coconut flour
- 2 large eggs, whisked
- ½ cup granular erythritol
- 1 teaspoon baking powder
- 1 teaspoon vanilla extract
- ½ cup sour cream

Directions:
1. Mix all ingredients in a large bowl. Pour batter into an ungreased 6" round nonstick baking dish.
2. Place baking dish into air fryer basket. Adjust the temperature to 300°F and set the timer for 25 minutes. The cake will be dark golden on top, and a toothpick inserted in the center should come out clean when done.
3. Let cool in dish 15 minutes before slicing and serving.

Roasted Pumpkin Seeds & Cinnamon

Servings: 2
Cooking Time: 35 Minutes
Ingredients:
- 1 cup pumpkin raw seeds
- 1 tbsp. ground cinnamon
- 2 tbsp. sugar
- 1 cup water
- 1 tbsp. olive oil

Directions:
1. In a frying pan, combine the pumpkin seeds, cinnamon and water.
2. Boil the mixture over a high heat for 2 - 3 minutes.
3. Pour out the water and place the seeds on a clean kitchen towel, allowing them to dry for 20 - 30 minutes.
4. In a bowl, mix together the sugar, dried seeds, a pinch of cinnamon and one tablespoon of olive oil.
5. Pre-heat the Air Fryer to 340°F.
6. Place the seed mixture in the fryer basket and allow to cook for 15 minutes, shaking the basket periodically throughout.

No Flour Lime Muffins

Servings:6
Cooking Time: 30 Minutes
Ingredients:
- Juice and zest of 2 limes
- 1 cup yogurt
- ¼ cup superfine sugar
- 8 oz cream cheese
- 1 tsp vanilla extract

Directions:
1. Preheat the air fryer to 330°F, and with a spatula, gently combine the yogurt and cheese. In another bowl, beat together the rest of the ingredients. Gently fold the lime with the cheese mixture. Divide the batter between 6 lined muffin tins. Cook in the air fryer for 10 minutes.

Glazed Chocolate Doughnut Holes

Servings: 5
Cooking Time: 22 Minutes
Ingredients:
- 1 cup self-rising flour
- 1 ¼ cups plain full-fat Greek yogurt
- ¼ cup cocoa powder
- ½ cup granulated sugar
- 1 cup confectioners' sugar
- ¼ cup heavy cream
- 1 teaspoon vanilla extract

Directions:
1. Preheat the air fryer to 350°F. Spray the inside of the air fryer basket with cooking spray.
2. In a large bowl, combine flour, yogurt, cocoa powder, and granulated sugar. Knead by hand 5 minutes until a large, sticky ball of dough is formed.
3. Roll mixture into balls, about 2 tablespoons each, to make twenty doughnut holes. Place doughnut holes in the air fryer basket and cook 12 minutes, working in batches as necessary.
4. While doughnut holes are cooking, in a medium bowl, mix confectioners' sugar, cream, and vanilla. Allow doughnut holes 5 minutes to cool before rolling each in the glaze. Chill in the refrigerator 5 minutes to allow glaze to set before serving.

Dark Chocolate Peanut Butter S'mores

Servings: 4
Cooking Time: 6 Minutes
Ingredients:
- 4 graham cracker sheets
- 4 marshmallows
- 4 teaspoons chunky peanut butter
- 4 ounces dark chocolate
- ½ teaspoon ground cinnamon

Directions:
1. Preheat the air fryer to 390°F. Break the graham crackers in half so you have 8 pieces.
2. Place 4 pieces of graham cracker on the bottom of the air fryer. Top each with one of the marshmallows and bake for 6 or 7 minutes, or until the marshmallows have a golden brown center.
3. While cooking, slather each of the remaining graham crackers with 1 teaspoon peanut butter.
4. When baking completes, carefully remove each of the graham crackers, add 1 ounce of dark chocolate on top of the marshmallow, and lightly sprinkle with cinnamon. Top with the remaining peanut butter graham cracker to make the sandwich. Serve immediately.

Peanut Butter S'mores

Servings:10
Cooking Time: 1 Minute
Ingredients:
- 10 Graham crackers (full, double-square cookies as they come out of the package)
- 5 tablespoons Natural-style creamy or crunchy peanut butter
- ½ cup Milk chocolate chips
- 10 Standard-size marshmallows (not minis and not jumbo campfire ones)

Directions:
1. Preheat the air fryer to 350°F .
2. Break the graham crackers in half widthwise at the marked place, so the rectangle is now in two squares. Set half of the squares flat side up on your work surface. Spread each with about 1½ teaspoons peanut butter, then set 10 to 12 chocolate chips point side up into the peanut butter on each, pressing gently so the chips stick.
3. Flatten a marshmallow between your clean, dry hands and set it atop the chips. Do the same with the remaining marshmallows on the other coated graham

crackers. Do not set the other half of the graham crackers on top of these coated graham crackers.

4. When the machine is at temperature, set the treats graham cracker side down in a single layer in the basket. They may touch, but even a fraction of an inch between them will provide better air flow. Air-fry undisturbed for 45 seconds.

5. Use a nonstick-safe spatula to transfer the topped graham crackers to a wire rack. Set the other graham cracker squares flat side down over the marshmallows. Cool for a couple of minutes before serving.

Sweet Potato Pie Rolls

Servings:3
Cooking Time: 8 Minutes
Ingredients:
- 6 Spring roll wrappers
- 1½ cups Canned yams in syrup, drained
- 2 tablespoons Light brown sugar
- ¼ teaspoon Ground cinnamon
- 1 Large egg(s), well beaten
- Vegetable oil spray

Directions:
1. Preheat the air fryer to 400°F.
2. Set a spring roll wrapper on a clean, dry work surface. Scoop up ¼ cup of the pulpy yams and set along one edge of the wrapper, leaving 2 inches on each side of the yams. Top the yams with about 1 teaspoon brown sugar and a pinch of ground cinnamon. Fold the sides of the wrapper perpendicular to the yam filling up and over the filling, partially covering it. Brush beaten egg(s) over the side of the wrapper farthest from the yam. Starting with the yam end, roll the wrapper closed, ending at the part with the beaten egg that you can press gently to seal. Lightly coat the roll on all sides with vegetable oil spray. Set it aside seam side down and continue filling, rolling, and spraying the remaining wrappers in the same way.
3. Set the rolls seam side down in the basket with as much air space between them as possible. Air-fry undisturbed for 8 minutes, or until crisp and golden brown.
4. Use a nonstick-safe spatula and perhaps kitchen tongs for balance to gently transfer the rolls to a wire rack. Cool for at least 5 minutes or up to 30 minutes before serving.

Molten Lava Cakes

Servings:3
Cooking Time: 10 Minutes

Ingredients:
- 2 large eggs
- 1 teaspoon vanilla extract
- ¼ teaspoon salt
- 3 tablespoons unsalted butter
- ¾ cup milk chocolate chips
- ¼ cup all-purpose flour
- Cooking spray

Directions:
1. Preheat the air fryer to 350°F. Spray three 4" ramekins with cooking spray.
2. In a medium bowl, whisk eggs, vanilla, and salt until well combined.
3. In a large microwave-safe bowl, microwave butter and chocolate chips in 20-second intervals, stirring after each interval, until mixture is fully melted, smooth, and pourable.
4. Whisk chocolate and slowly add egg mixture. Whisk until fully combined.
5. Sprinkle flour into bowl and whisk into chocolate mixture. It should be easily pourable.
6. Divide batter evenly among prepared ramekins. Place in the air fryer basket and cook 5 minutes until the edges and top are set.
7. Let cool 5 minutes and use a butter knife to loosen the edges from ramekins.
8. To serve, place a small dessert plate upside down on top of each ramekin. Quickly flip ramekin and plate upside down so lava cake drops to the plate. Let cool 5 minutes. Serve.

Apple Pie Crumble

Servings:4
Cooking Time:25 Minutes
Ingredients:
- 1 can apple pie
- ¼ cup butter, softened
- 9 tablespoons self-rising flour
- 7 tablespoons caster sugar
- Pinch of salt

Directions:
1. Preheat the Air fryer to 320°F and grease a baking dish.
2. Mix all the ingredients in a bowl until a crumbly mixture is formed.
3. Arrange the apple pie in the baking dish and top with the mixture.
4. Transfer the baking dish into the Air fryer basket and cook for about 25 minutes.
5. Dish out in a platter and serve.

Pumpkin Pie

Servings:6
Cooking Time: 2 Hours 25 Minutes
Ingredients:
- 1 can pumpkin pie mix
- 1 large egg
- 1 teaspoon vanilla extract
- ⅓ cup sweetened condensed milk
- 1 premade graham cracker piecrust

Directions:
1. Preheat the air fryer to 325°F.
2. In a large bowl, whisk together pumpkin pie mix, egg, vanilla, and sweetened condensed milk until well combined. Pour mixture into piecrust.
3. Place in the air fryer basket and cook 25 minutes until pie is brown, firm, and a toothpick inserted into the center comes out clean.
4. Chill in the refrigerator until set, at least 2 hours, before serving.

Lime Bars

Servings:12
Cooking Time: 33 Minutes
Ingredients:
- 1½ cups blanched finely ground almond flour, divided
- ¾ cup confectioners' erythritol, divided
- 4 tablespoons salted butter, melted
- ½ cup fresh lime juice
- 2 large eggs, whisked

Directions:
1. In a medium bowl, mix together 1 cup flour, ¼ cup erythritol, and butter. Press mixture into bottom of an ungreased 6" round nonstick cake pan.
2. Place pan into air fryer basket. Adjust the temperature to 300°F and set the timer for 13 minutes. Crust will be brown and set in the middle when done.
3. Allow to cool in pan 10 minutes.
4. In a medium bowl, combine remaining flour, remaining erythritol, lime juice, and eggs. Pour mixture over cooled crust and return to air fryer for 20 minutes at 300°F. Top will be browned and firm when done.
5. Let cool completely in pan, about 30 minutes, then chill covered in the refrigerator 1 hour. Serve chilled.

Chocolate Soufflés

Servings:2
Cooking Time: 15 Minutes

Ingredients:
- 2 large eggs, whites and yolks separated
- 1 teaspoon vanilla extract
- 2 ounces low-carb chocolate chips
- 2 teaspoons coconut oil, melted

Directions:
1. In a medium bowl, beat egg whites until stiff peaks form, about 2 minutes. Set aside. In a separate medium bowl, whisk egg yolks and vanilla together. Set aside.
2. In a separate medium microwave-safe bowl, place chocolate chips and drizzle with coconut oil. Microwave on high 20 seconds, then stir and continue cooking in 10-second increments until melted, being careful not to overheat chocolate. Let cool 1 minute.
3. Slowly pour melted chocolate into egg yolks and whisk until smooth. Then, slowly begin adding egg white mixture to chocolate mixture, about ¼ cup at a time, folding in gently.
4. Pour mixture into two 4" ramekins greased with cooking spray. Place ramekins into air fryer basket. Adjust the temperature to 400°F and set the timer for 15 minutes. Soufflés will puff up while cooking and deflate a little once cooled. The center will be set when done. Let cool 10 minutes, then serve warm.

Chocolate-covered Maple Bacon

Servings: 4
Cooking Time: 25 Minutes
Ingredients:
- 8 slices sugar-free bacon
- 1 tbsp. granular erythritol
- 1/3 cup low-carb sugar-free chocolate chips
- 1 tsp. coconut oil
- ½ tsp. maple extract

Directions:
1. Place the bacon in the fryer's basket and add the erythritol on top. Cook for six minutes at 350°F and turn the bacon over. Leave to cook another six minutes or until the bacon is sufficiently crispy.
2. Take the bacon out of the fryer and leave it to cool.
3. Microwave the chocolate chips and coconut oil together for half a minute. Remove from the microwave and mix together before stirring in the maple extract.
4. Set the bacon flat on a piece of parchment paper and pour the mixture over. Allow to harden in the refrigerator for roughly five minutes before serving.

Baked Apple

Servings: 6
Cooking Time: 20 Minutes
Ingredients:

- 3 small Honey Crisp or other baking apples
- 3 tablespoons maple syrup
- 3 tablespoons chopped pecans
- 1 tablespoon firm butter, cut into 6 pieces

Directions:

1. Put ½ cup water in the drawer of the air fryer.
2. Wash apples well and dry them.
3. Split apples in half. Remove core and a little of the flesh to make a cavity for the pecans.
4. Place apple halves in air fryer basket, cut side up.
5. Spoon 1½ teaspoons pecans into each cavity.
6. Spoon ½ tablespoon maple syrup over pecans in each apple.
7. Top each apple with ½ teaspoon butter.
8. Cook at 360°F for 20 minutes, until apples are tender.

Ricotta Lemon Cake

Servings: 8
Cooking Time: 40 Minutes
Ingredients:

- 1 lb ricotta
- 4 eggs
- 1 lemon juice
- 1 lemon zest
- ¼ cup erythritol

Directions:

1. Preheat the air fryer to 325°F.
2. Spray air fryer baking dish with cooking spray.
3. In a bowl, beat ricotta cheese until smooth.
4. Whisk in the eggs one by one.
5. Whisk in lemon juice and zest.
6. Pour batter into the prepared baking dish and place into the air fryer.
7. Cook for 40 minutes.
8. Allow to cool completely then slice and serve.

Sage Cream

Servings: 4
Cooking Time: 30 Minutes
Ingredients:

- 7 cups red currants
- 1 cup swerve
- 1 cup water
- 6 sage leaves

Directions:

1. In a pan that fits your air fryer, mix all the ingredients, toss, put the pan in the fryer and cook at 330°F for 30 minutes. Discard sage leaves, divide into cups and serve cold.

Brown Sugar Baked Apples

Servings: 4
Cooking Time: 15 Minutes
Ingredients:

- 3 Small tart apples, preferably McIntosh
- 4 tablespoons (¼ cup/½ stick) Butter
- 6 tablespoons Light brown sugar
- Ground cinnamon
- Table salt

Directions:

1. Preheat the air fryer to 400°F.
2. Stem the apples, then cut them in half through their "equators". Use a melon baller to core the apples, taking care not to break through the flesh and skin at any point but creating a little well in the center of each half.
3. When the machine is at temperature, remove the basket and set it on a heat-safe work surface. Set the apple halves cut side up in the basket with as much air space between them as possible. Even a fraction of an inch will work. Drop 2 teaspoons of butter into the well in the center of each apple half. Sprinkle each half with 1 tablespoon brown sugar and a pinch each ground cinnamon and table salt.
4. Return the basket to the machine. Air-fry undisturbed for 15 minutes, or until the apple halves have softened and the brown sugar has caramelized.
5. Use a nonstick-safe spatula to transfer the apple halves cut side up to a wire rack. Cool for at least 10 minutes before serving, or serve at room temperature.

Coconut And Berries Cream

Servings: 6
Cooking Time: 30 Minutes
Ingredients:

- 12 ounces blackberries
- 6 ounces raspberries
- 12 ounces blueberries
- ¾ cup swerve
- 2 ounces coconut cream

Directions:

1. In a bowl, mix all the ingredients and whisk well. Divide this into 6 ramekins, put them in your air fryer and cook at 320°F for 30 minutes. Cool down and serve it.

Delicious Spiced Apples

Servings: 6
Cooking Time: 10 Minutes
Ingredients:
- 4 small apples, sliced
- 1 tsp apple pie spice
- 1/2 cup erythritol
- 2 tbsp coconut oil, melted

Directions:
1. Add apple slices in a mixing bowl and sprinkle sweetener, apple pie spice, and coconut oil over apple and toss to coat.
2. Transfer apple slices in air fryer dish. Place dish in air fryer basket and cook at 350°F for 10 minutes.
3. Serve and enjoy.

Easy Mug Brownie

Servings: 1
Cooking Time: 10 Minutes
Ingredients:
- 1 scoop chocolate protein powder
- 1 tbsp cocoa powder
- 1/2 tsp baking powder
- 1/4 cup unsweetened almond milk

Directions:
1. Add baking powder, protein powder, and cocoa powder in a mug and mix well.
2. Add milk in a mug and stir well.
3. Place the mug in the air fryer and cook at 390°F for 10 minutes.
4. Serve and enjoy.

Monkey Bread

Servings: 6
Cooking Time: 20 Minutes
Ingredients:
- 1 can refrigerated biscuit dough
- ½ cup granulated sugar
- 1 tablespoon ground cinnamon
- ¼ cup salted butter, melted
- ¼ cup brown sugar
- Cooking spray

Directions:
1. Preheat the air fryer to 325°F. Spray a 6" round cake pan with cooking spray. Separate biscuits and cut each into four pieces.
2. In a large bowl, stir granulated sugar with cinnamon. Toss biscuit pieces in the cinnamon and sugar mixture until well coated. Place each biscuit piece in prepared pan.
3. In a medium bowl, stir together butter and brown sugar. Pour mixture evenly over the biscuit pieces.
4. Place pan in the air fryer basket and cook 20 minutes until brown. Let cool 10 minutes before flipping bread out of the pan and serving.

Cherry Cheesecake Rolls

Servings: 6
Cooking Time: 30 Minutes
Ingredients:
- 1 can crescent rolls
- 4 oz cream cheese
- 1 tbsp cherry preserves
- 1/3 cup sliced fresh cherries
- Cooking spray

Directions:
1. Roll out the dough into a large rectangle on a flat work surface. Cut the dough into 12 rectangles by cutting 3 cuts across and 2 cuts down. In a microwave-safe bowl, soften cream cheese for 15 seconds. Stir together with cherry preserves. Mound 2 tsp of the cherries-cheese mix on each piece of dough. Carefully spread the mixture but not on the edges. Top with 2 tsp of cherries each. Roll each triangle to make a cylinder.
2. Preheat air fryer to 350°F. Place the first batch of the rolls in the greased air fryer. Spray the rolls with cooking oil and Bake for 8 minutes. Let cool in the air fryer for 2-3 minutes before removing. Serve.

Crème Brulee

Servings: 3
Cooking Time: 60 Minutes
Ingredients:
- 1 cup milk
- 2 vanilla pods
- 10 egg yolks
- 4 tbsp sugar + extra for topping

Directions:
1. In a pan, add the milk and cream. Cut the vanilla pods open and scrape the seeds into the pan with the vanilla pods also. Place the pan over medium heat on a stovetop until almost boiled while stirring regularly. Turn off the heat. Add the egg yolks to a bowl and beat it. Add the sugar and mix well but not too bubbly.
2. Remove the vanilla pods from the milk mixture; pour the mixture onto the eggs mixture while stirring constantly. Let it sit for 25 minutes. Fill 2 to 3 ramekins with the mixture. Place the ramekins in the fryer basket and cook them at 190°F for 50 minutes. Once ready, remove the ramekins and let sit to cool. Sprinkle the remaining sugar over and use a torch to melt the sugar, so it browns at the top.

Apple Pie

Servings: 7
Cooking Time: 25 Minutes
Ingredients:

- 2 large apples
- ½ cup flour
- 2 tbsp. unsalted butter
- 1 tbsp. sugar
- ½ tsp. cinnamon

Directions:

1. Pre-heat the Air Fryer to 360°F
2. In a large bowl, combine the flour and butter. Pour in the sugar, continuing to mix.
3. Add in a few tablespoons of water and combine everything to create a smooth dough.
4. Grease the insides of a few small pastry tins with butter. Divide the dough between each tin and lay each portion flat inside.
5. Peel, core and dice up the apples. Put the diced apples on top of the pastry and top with a sprinkling of sugar and cinnamon.
6. Place the pastry tins in your Air Fryer and cook for 15 - 17 minutes.
7. Serve.

Glazed Donuts

Servings: 2 – 4
Cooking Time: 25 Minutes
Ingredients:

- 1 can [8 oz.] refrigerated croissant dough
- Cooking spray
- 1 can [16 oz.] vanilla frosting

Directions:

1. Cut the croissant dough into 1-inch-round slices. Make a hole in the center of each one to create a donut.
2. Put the donuts in the Air Fryer basket, taking care not to overlap any, and spritz with cooking spray. You may need to cook everything in multiple batches.
3. Cook at 400°F for 2 minutes. Turn the donuts over and cook for another 3 minutes.
4. Place the rolls on a paper plate.
5. Microwave a half-cup of frosting for 30 seconds and pour a drizzling of the frosting over the donuts before serving.

Chocolate Brownie

Servings: 4
Cooking Time: 16 Minutes
Ingredients:

- 1 cup bananas, overripe
- 1 scoop protein powder
- 2 tbsp unsweetened cocoa powder
- 1/2 cup almond butter, melted

Directions:

1. Preheat the air fryer to 325°F.
2. Spray air fryer baking pan with cooking spray.
3. Add all ingredients into the blender and blend until smooth.
4. Pour batter into the prepared pan and place in the air fryer basket.
5. Cook brownie for 16 minutes.
6. Serve and enjoy.

Banana Chips With Chocolate Glaze

Servings: 2
Cooking Time: 20 Minutes
Ingredients:

- 2 banana, cut into slices
- 1/4 teaspoon lemon zest
- 1 tablespoon agave syrup
- 1 tablespoon cocoa powder
- 1 tablespoon coconut oil, melted

Directions:

1. Toss the bananas with the lemon zest and agave syrup. Transfer your bananas to the parchment-lined cooking basket.
2. Bake in the preheated Air Fryer at 370°F for 12 minutes, turning them over halfway through the cooking time.
3. In the meantime, melt the coconut oil in your microwave; add the cocoa powder and whisk to combine well.
4. Serve the baked banana chips. Enjoy!

Fried Twinkies

Servings:6
Cooking Time: 5 Minutes
Ingredients:

- 2 Large egg white(s)
- 2 tablespoons Water
- 1½ cups Ground gingersnap cookie crumbs
- 6 Twinkies
- Vegetable oil spray

Directions:

1. Preheat the air fryer to 400°F.
2. Set up and fill two shallow soup plates or small pie plates on your counter: one for the egg white(s),

whisked with the water until foamy; and one for the gingersnap crumbs.

3. Dip a Twinkie in the egg white(s), turning it to coat on all sides, even the ends. Let the excess egg white mixture slip back into the rest, then set the Twinkie in the crumbs. Roll it to coat on all sides, even the ends, pressing gently to get an even coating. Then repeat this process: egg white(s), followed by crumbs. Lightly coat the prepared Twinkie on all sides with vegetable oil spray. Set aside and coat each of the remaining Twinkies with the same double-dipping technique, followed by spraying.

4. Set the Twinkies flat side up in the basket with as much air space between them as possible. Air-fry for 5 minutes, or until browned and crunchy.

5. Use a nonstick-safe spatula to gently transfer the Twinkies to a wire rack. Cool for at least 10 minutes before serving.

Cream Cheese Shortbread Cookies

Servings:12
Cooking Time: 20 Minutes
Ingredients:
- ¼ cup coconut oil, melted
- 2 ounces cream cheese, softened
- ½ cup granular erythritol
- 1 large egg, whisked
- 2 cups blanched finely ground almond flour
- 1 teaspoon almond extract

Directions:
1. Combine all ingredients in a large bowl to form a firm ball.
2. Place dough on a sheet of plastic wrap and roll into a 12"-long log shape. Roll log in plastic wrap and place in refrigerator 30 minutes to chill.
3. Remove log from plastic and slice into twelve equal cookies. Cut two sheets of parchment paper to fit air fryer basket. Place six cookies on each ungreased sheet. Place one sheet with cookies into air fryer basket. Adjust the temperature to 320°F and set the timer for 10 minutes, turning cookies halfway through cooking. They will be lightly golden when done. Repeat with remaining cookies.
4. Let cool 15 minutes before serving to avoid crumbling.

Fiesta Pastries

Servings:8
Cooking Time:20 Minutes
Ingredients:

- ½ of apple, peeled, cored and chopped
- 1 teaspoon fresh orange zest, grated finely
- 7.05-ounce prepared frozen puff pastry, cut into 16 squares
- ½ tablespoon white sugar
- ½ teaspoon ground cinnamon

Directions:
1. Preheat the Air fryer to 390°F and grease an Air fryer basket.
2. Mix all ingredients in a bowl except puff pastry.
3. Arrange about 1 teaspoon of this mixture in the center of each square.
4. Fold each square into a triangle and slightly press the edges with a fork.
5. Arrange the pastries in the Air fryer basket and cook for about 10 minutes.
6. Dish out and serve immediately.

Cranberries Pudding

Servings: 6
Cooking Time: 20 Minutes
Ingredients:
- 1 cup cauliflower rice
- 2 cups almond milk
- ½ cup cranberries
- 1 teaspoon vanilla extract

Directions:
1. In a pan that fits your air fryer, mix all the ingredients, whisk a bit, put the pan in the fryer and cook at 360°F for 20 minutes. Stir the pudding, divide into bowls and serve cold.

Chocolate Chip Cookie Cake

Servings:8
Cooking Time: 15 Minutes
Ingredients:
- 4 tablespoons salted butter, melted
- ⅓ cup granular brown erythritol
- 1 large egg
- ½ teaspoon vanilla extract
- 1 cup blanched finely ground almond flour
- ½ teaspoon baking powder
- ¼ cup low-carb chocolate chips

Directions:
1. In a large bowl, whisk together butter, erythritol, egg, and vanilla. Add flour and baking powder, and stir until combined.
2. Fold in chocolate chips, then spoon batter into an ungreased 6" round nonstick baking dish.
3. Place dish into air fryer basket. Adjust the temperature to 300°F and set the timer for 15 minutes. When edges are browned, cookie cake will be done.
4. Slice and serve warm.

RECIPES INDEX

Printed in Great Britain
by Amazon

22383702R00059